STUDY NOTES
Samuel Taylor Coleridge
Selected Poems

FOR OCR A-LEVEL

CHRIS WEBSTER

PASSPORT
STUDY NOTES

DEDICATION

To all the pupils I have ever taught, beginning at Rotherham Girls' High School, and including such highs and lows as Riddings Comprehensive School, Scunthorpe, and Saltus Grammar School, Bermuda (I won't say which was the high and which was the low because both had both), and my latest and most exotic, an international school in Singapore —I won't name it, because I don't want my readers popping in for an autograph (or to get their money back).

CONTENTS

INTRODUCTION

These study notes were written for the OCR syllabus H472, Version 1.3 (September 2018). They include the full text of all the set poems, glossaries, questions on the poems, commentaries, essays on themes, sample examination questions, and a brief biography.

A unique feature of these notes is the "lite" version of the longer poems. These are abridged versions (by omitting some of the text and replacing it with short prose summaries) which can be used as a first step in the study of the complete poems, the text of which, along with further questions and notes, is also included.

The study notes are suitable for both individual and class use. When used in class, one approach would be read the poem with the students then ask them to work through the questions in pairs or small groups. When they have finished, discuss their responses. Only then should the commentaries be read and discussed. On occasions students could be asked to follow up the lesson with different kinds of writing. Sometimes this will be a response to some or all of the questions. Sometimes they could be asked to write their own commentary on a poem (without reading the commentary in the book).

The essay and examination questions at the end of the book can be used in a number of ways: students could be asked to present an essay topic to the class, for example, in a PowerPoint presentation. They can also be used for homework essays and practice under examination conditions.

THE AEOLIAN HARP

COMPOSED AT CLEVEDON, SOMERSETSHIRE

My pensive Sara! thy soft cheek reclined
Thus on mine arm, most soothing sweet it is
To sit beside our Cot, our Cot o'ergrown
With white-flower'd Jasmin, and the broad-leav'd Myrtle,
(Meet emblems they of Innocence and Love!)   5
And watch the clouds, that late were rich with light,
Slow saddening round, and mark the star of eve
Serenely brilliant (such should Wisdom be)
Shine opposite! How exquisite the scents
Snatch'd from yon bean-field! and the world *so* hush'd! 10
The stilly murmur of the distant Sea
Tells us of silence.

    And that simplest Lute,
Placed length-ways in the clasping casement, hark!
How by the desultory breeze caress'd,
Like some coy maid half yielding to her lover,   15
It pours such sweet upbraiding, as must needs
Tempt to repeat the wrong! And now, its strings
Boldlier swept, the long sequacious notes
Over delicious surges sink and rise,
Such a soft floating witchery of sound   20
As twilight Elfins make, when they at eve

Voyage on gentle gales from Fairy-Land,
Where Melodies round honey-dropping flowers,
Footless and wild, like birds of Paradise,
Nor pause, nor perch, hovering on untam'd wing!   25
O! the one Life within us and abroad,
Which meets all motion and becomes its soul,
A light in sound, a sound-like power in light,
Rhythm in all thought, and joyance every where—
Methinks, it should have been impossible   30
Not to love all things in a world so fill'd;
Where the breeze warbles, and the mute still air
Is Music slumbering on her instrument.

   And thus, my Love! as on the midway slope
Of yonder hill I stretch my limbs at noon,   35
Whilst through my half-closed eye-lids I behold
The sunbeams dance, like diamonds, on the main,
And tranquil muse upon tranquillity;
Full many a thought uncall'd and undetain'd,
And many idle flitting phantasies,   40
Traverse my indolent and passive brain,
As wild and various as the random gales
That swell and flutter on this subject Lute!

   And what if all of animated nature
Be but organic Harps diversely fram'd,   45
That tremble into thought, as o'er them sweeps
Plastic and vast, one intellectual breeze,
At once the Soul of each, and God of all?

   But thy more serious eye a mild reproof
Darts, O belovéd Woman! nor such thoughts   50
Dim and unhallow'd dost thou not reject,
And biddest me walk humbly with my God.
Meek Daughter in the family of Christ!
Well hast thou said and holily disprais'd
These shapings of the unregenerate mind;   55
Bubbles that glitter as they rise and break
On vain Philosophy's aye-babbling spring.
For never guiltless may I speak of him,

The Incomprehensible! save when with awe
I praise him, and with Faith that inly *feels*;   60
Who with his saving mercies healéd me,
A sinful and most miserable man,
Wilder'd and dark, and gave me to possess
Peace, and this Cot, and thee, heart-honour'd Maid!

(1795)

GLOSSARY

aeolian harp – a stringed instrument played by the wind.
cot – cottage.
casement – a window that opens on hinges.
desultory – lacking in purpose.
coy – pretending to be shy.
upbraiding – finding fault with.
sequacious – in sequence.
joyance – joy.
plastic – flexible.
unregenerate – not revived or renewed.

QUESTIONS

The poem is addressed to Sara Fricker who was soon to become his wife (they were married on 4th October, 1795). Pick out words and phrases that show his love for her.

How does Coleridge describe the Aeolian harp? Look at his use of adjectives, adverbs, and particularly at the simile in line 15. Explain the effect of this simile and examine how it is extended over the next line and a half.

What does the word "witchery" mean, and how does Coleridge develop the idea in the next five lines?

What other beauties of nature does Coleridge describe in this poem?

In lines 26 to 31, and 44 to 48, Coleridge expresses his Pantheistic philosophy (Pantheistic means that God is in all things, particularly in Nature). Try to explain his ideas in simple words.

In the last section of the poem, lines 49 – 64, Coleridge answers for Sara, reflecting her objections to his Pantheism because of her traditional Christianity. Express her objects in simple terms.

Does Coleridge accept her point of view? What is the evidence?

The Aeolian Harp is the first in a group of poems classified as "Conversation Poems" because of their conversational style. Find phrases which reflect this style.

Sara's replies are suggested in Coleridge's own words. Choose a section from the poem and write it as a conversation, for example:

COL: What if all nature had one soul and that soul was God?
SARA: That's a crazy idea! You should walk humbly with the Christian God that you learn about in church.
COL: Well said. My thoughts deserve criticism because they are as meaningless as the bubbles of a spring.
SARA: You should have Faith.
COL: You are right! I praise God because he has given me peace, this cottage, and you, my love.

The poem is written in free-flowing iambic pentameters. Analyse a few lines by marking the five stressed syllables as follows:

   /   /   /   /   /
My Pensive Sara! Thy soft cheek reclined

Can you find many irregular lines? (for example, line 29). Compare with Shakespeare's blank verse, which has many irregularities. Discuss the effect of each.

Choose two or three words which describe the tone of the poem.

COMMENTARY

The Eolian Harp (Coleridge's spelling) is one of a group of poems which are usually classified as "Conversation Poems". The other poems in this group are: *Reflections on having left a Place of Retirement, This Lime-Tree Bower my Prison, Frost at Midnight, Fears in Solitude, The Nightingale, Dejection: an Ode* and *To William Wordsworth.*

They are conversational in style and tone, even though they are not actual conversations. The language is the everyday language of the poet and is very different from what Coleridge later termed: 'Gaudyverse'

Let us consider what he meant by this term from the *An Essay on Criticism* by one of the great poets of the previous generation, Alexander Pope (1688-1744). In this passage, Pope is criticising incompetent poets, so we can see the style at its worst:

In the bright Muse tho' thousand Charms conspire,
Her Voice is all these tuneful Fools admire,
Who haunt Parnassus but to please their Ear,
Not mend their Minds; as some to Church repair,
Not for the Doctrine, but the Musick there.
These Equal Syllables alone require,
Tho' oft the Ear the open Vowels tire,
While Expletives their feeble Aid do join,
And ten low Words oft creep in one dull Line,
While they ring round the same unvary'd Chimes,
With sure Returns of still expected Rhymes.
Where-e'er you find the cooling Western Breeze,
In the next Line, it whispers thro' the Trees;
If Chrystal Streams with pleasing Murmurs creep,
The Reader's threaten'd (not in vain) with Sleep.
Then, at the last, and only Couplet fraught
With some unmeaning Thing they call a Thought,
A needless Alexandrine ends the Song,
That like a wounded Snake, drags its slow length along.

The following features are worth noting:

- The poem is written in 'heroic couplets' – iambic pentameter rhyming couplets.
- Much use is made of Classical allusions. In this example we have 'Parnassus'.
- Poems were expected to rhyme, but the rhymes were overused and tired.
- There was a specialised 'poetic diction', here exemplified by 'Chrystal Streams'.
- Narrative poems often ended with a six-stress line called an Alexandrine. Pope is here referring to a mindless adherence to rules whether they were effective or not.

The overall effect is poetry which is highly formalised and artificial, but the Romantics were striving for something which was less formal and completely natural. This was best expressed at a later date in the *Preface to the Lyrical Ballads* in the phrase: "language of men".

Coleridge has achieved this par excellence. His iambic pentameters, though fairly strict in metre, have the rhythm of natural speech. The language, if not "language of men" is close to the language that Coleridge would use in his everyday conversation. This is something new in poetry, but from our 21st century perspective, after more than 100 years of free verse, it is easy for us to miss it. If time allows, it would be most valuable for students to sample the "poetic diction" in a selection of 18th century verse. A good starting point would be the example by Thomas Gray that Wordsworth gave in the *Preface to the Lyrical Ballads* (1800):

In vain to me the smiling mornings shine,
And reddening Phœbus lifts his golden fire:
The birds in vain their amorous descant join,
Or cheerful fields resume their green attire.
These ears, alas! for other notes repine;
A different object do these eyes require;
My lonely anguish melts no heart but mine;
And in my breast the imperfect joys expire;
Yet morning smiles the busy race to cheer,

And new-born pleasure brings to happier men;
The fields to all their wonted tribute bear;
To warm their little loves the birds complain.
I fruitless mourn to him that cannot hear,
And weep the more because I weep in vain.

The Aeolian Harp is addressed to Sara Fricker in just before their marriage in 1795, and is in some respects a love poem. We see this in the first two lines, line 34, and the respect he shows for her conventional views on religion in lines 49 to the end. The final words of the poem are words of love: "heart-honoured Maid!"

However, the most important topic in the poem is the Aeolian harp, as it is from his reflections on its sound that all the ideas in the poem arise. His description begins with a surprising simile. Its sound is compared to "some coy maid half yielding to her lover" (line 15). This suggests the slow way in which the strings respond to the wind. The simile is extended in the following lines with the oxymoron "sweet upbraiding". In simple terms, the protests of the woman are so sweet as to be inviting. The strings are now swept "boldlier" – an unusual comparative form of the adjective 'boldly'.

He goes on the describe the sounds as "witchery", a word with interesting connotations. The most important for Coleridge is the idea of magic. A witch was a mythical creature found in folk tales, and he develops this idea with references to "Elfins" and "Fairy-Land". It is the magical enchantment that he wishes to emphasise rather than any of the more sinister connotations of the word "witch". The next two lines are a brief description of "Fairy-Land" and seem to describe music and beautiful flowers which fly like birds – a strange but beautiful description. This leads into the philosophical section described above.

Nature is an important secondary theme in the poem, as can be seen in the first section in which Coleridge describes the scene around his 'Cot': he mentions "Jasmin, Myrtle, clouds, light and "the star of eve". There is a nice, homely touch in his reference to "yon beanfield".

It is interesting that, in this poem, in which the sound of the

Aeolian harp and beauties of nature lead to pantheistic reflections, he is anticipating by three years Wordsworth's achievement in *Tintern Abbey* (1798).

REFLECTIONS ON HAVING LEFT A PLACE OF RETIREMENT

Sermoni propriora.–HOR.

Low was our pretty Cot: our tallest Rose
Peep'd at the chamber-window. We could hear
At silent noon, and eve, and early morn,
The Sea's faint murmur. In the open air
Our Myrtles blossom'd; and across the porch   5
Thick Jasmins twined: the little landscape round
Was green and woody, and refresh'd the eye.
It was a spot which you might aptly call
The Valley of Seclusion! Once I saw
(Hallowing his Sabbath-day by quietness)   10
A wealthy son of Commerce saunter by,
Bristowa's citizen: methought, it calm'd
His thirst of idle gold, and made him muse
With wiser feelings: for he paus'd, and look'd
With a pleas'd sadness, and gaz'd all around,   15
Then eyed our Cottage, and gaz'd round again,
And sigh'd, and said, it was a Blesséd Place.
And we *were* bless'd. Oft with patient ear
Long-listening to the viewless sky-lark's note
(Viewless, or haply for a moment seen   20
Gleaming on sunny wings) in whisper'd tones
I've said to my Belovéd, 'Such, sweet Girl!

The inobtrusive song of Happiness,
Unearthly minstrelsy! then only heard
When the Soul seeks to hear; when all is hush'd,   25
And the Heart listens!'

       But the time, when first
From that low Dell, steep up the stony Mount
I climb'd with perilous toil and reach'd the top,
Oh! what a goodly scene! *Here* the bleak mount,
The bare bleak mountain speckled thin with sheep;   30
Grey clouds, that shadowing spot the sunny fields;
And river, now with bushy rocks o'er-brow'd,
Now winding bright and full, with naked banks;
And seats, and lawns, the Abbey and the wood,
And cots, and hamlets, and faint city-spire;   35
The Channel *there*, the Islands and white sails,
Dim coasts, and cloud-like hills, and shoreless Ocean –
It seem'd like Omnipresence! God, methought,
Had built him there a Temple: the whole World
Seem'd *imag'd* in its vast circumference: 40
No *wish* profan'd my overwhelméd heart.
Blest hour! It was a luxury, – to be!

  Ah! quiet Dell! dear Cot, and Mount sublime!
I was constrain'd to quit you. Was it right,
While my unnumber'd brethren toil'd and bled,   45
That I should dream away the entrusted hours
On rose-leaf beds, pampering the coward heart
With feelings all too delicate for use?
Sweet is the tear that from some Howard's eye
Drops on the cheek of one he lifts from earth: 50
And he that works me good with unmov'd face,
Does it but half: he chills me while he aids,
My benefactor, not my brother man!
Yet even this, this cold beneficence
Praise, praise it, O my Soul! oft as thou scann'st   55
The sluggard Pity's vision-weaving tribe!
Who sigh for Wretchedness, yet shun the Wretched,
Nursing in some delicious solitude
Their slothful loves and dainty sympathies!

I therefore go, and join head, heart, and hand,   60
Active and firm, to fight the bloodless fight
Of Science, Freedom, and the Truth in Christ.

Yet oft when after honourable toil
Bests the tir'd mind, and waking loves to dream,
My spirit shall revisit thee, dear Cot!   65
Thy Jasmin and thy window-peeping Rose,
And Myrtles fearless of the mild sea-air.
And I shall sigh fond wishes – sweet Abode!
Ah! – had none greater! And that all had such!
It might be so—but the time is not yet.   70
Speed it, O Father! Let thy Kingdom come!

  (1795)

GLOSSARY

Sermoni propriora – "more suitable to prose/conversation".
Bristowa – Bristol? Bristol was a thriving hub of industry and commerce.
viewless – unseen.
haply – perhaps.
Dell – a small, secluded valley.
o'er-browed – overhanging.
Howard – Henry Howard, the poet Earl of Surrey.
sluggard – a lazy person.

QUESTIONS

Read the note on page 5 about the group of poems to which this poem belongs, then comment on the epigraph, "Sermoni propriora" from the Latin poet, Horace.

Compare the description of the scene around his 'Cot" with the description in Aeolian Harp. What additional details are presented in this description?

How does the "wealthy son of Commerce" who "saunters by" respond these surroundings?

Why do you think Coleridge used the adjective "idle" with "gold" in line 13?

Explain the phrase "pleased sadness" in line 15. In what sense can it be considered an oxymoron?

How does he describe the skylark's song? What does it represent for him?

Make a list of what can be seen from the top of the "Mount"?

List some of the vivid adjectives used in the section from lines 27 – 42.

Check the meaning of the word "sublime" and discuss how it applies to this passage.

Check the meaning of the word "Pantheisism" and discuss whether the description could be applied to the religious reflections in lines 36 – 39.

Explain in your own words what Coleridge may have meant by line 42.

In lines 43 to 62 he explains why he feels that it is necessary for him to leave the place. Try to find at least three reasons.

Explain lines 55 to 57. How do they apply to Coleridge?

Compare and contrast lines 63 to 71 with this passage from Wordsworth's *Tintern Abbey*:

> These beauteous forms,
> Through a long absence, have not been to me
> As is a landscape to a blind man's eye:
> But oft, in lonely rooms, and mid the din
> Of towns and cities, I have owed to them,

In hours of weariness, sensations sweet
Felt in the blood, and felt along the heart;
And passing even into my purer mind,
With tranquil restoration.

(1798)

What main idea are the two poets expressing? Which poet, in your opinion, does it most effectively? Is there any evidence of Coleridge's influence in Wordsworth's poem?

Reread the explanation of the term "conversation poem" on page 4 and explore how it applies to this poem.

Imagine that Coleridge has a conversation with the "son of Commerce" and write it out. In your conversation, include a discussion of Coleridge's reasons for leaving.

Choose two or three words to describe the tone of the poem and explain why you chose them.

COMMENTARY

Coleridge presents his "Cot" to us in five sections:

1. straightforward description
2. seeing it through the yes of a "son of Commerce"
3. describing the landscape around it from the "stony Mount"
4. explaining his reasons for leaving it (lines 44 – 62)
5. saying how the memory of it will refresh his spirit

The key idea in this poem is expressed in section 4: Coleridge feels "constrained" to leave his "Cot" because of a sense of duty to help his "brother man" by playing a part in "the bloodless fight/ Of Science, Freedom, and the Truth in Christ."

The poem begins with an extended description of the beauty of the "Cot". It is surrounded by flowers and blossoms: "Rose",

"Myrtle" and "Jasmin" and it is set in a "green and woody" landscape, near the sea.

The beauty of the place is emphasised by seeing it through the eyes of a holidaying businessman ("a wealthy son of Commerce").

In lines 2 – 26 he tells us that he said to his "Beloved" that the skylark's song was the "song of Happiness" of a deeply spiritual type that affects the "Soul" and the "Heart" (emotions).

Lines 26 – 42 describe the landscape as he first saw it from the vantage point of the "Mount". The description has some characteristics of the sublime. (The **sublime** in literature is description that excites emotions beyond ordinary experience, for example, description of wild nature or scenes of grandeur). This can be found in words and phrases such as "bleak mount", "bare bleak mountain", "with bushy rocks o'er-browed", "Dim coasts, and cloud-like hills." etc. The awe and exaltation lead on to religious musings of a Pantheistic kind, expressed, for example, in the word "Omnipresence". This section ends with an expression of Zen-like awareness of the present moment. This section is a very fine example of the response to nature in the Romantic period and can equal anything produced by Wordsworth.

In lines 43 – 62, Coleridge addresses the matter which gives the poem its title; his reasons for leaving such a beautiful and happy place. He feels that it is his duty to play a part in the world, not the part played by the "son of Commerce", which is fundamentally selfish, a "thirst of idle gold", but a part which will serve mankind: "the bloodless fight/ Of Science, Freedom, and the Truth in Christ." Note the Christian element in this statement. Though Coleridge toys with Pantheism, his beliefs, perhaps because of his wife's influence, are those of traditional Christianity.

The last section of the poem bears a remarkable resemblance to a passage from Wordsworth's famous *Tintern Abbey* which was written three years later. They express the idea that the memory of his "dear Cot" will refresh him after "honourable toil".

The poem ends with a conventionally Christian wish that all

men might have such a "sweet Abode", and that they will, when God's Kingdom comes.

The poem has little imagery of the conventional kind, though we note the personification of the sound of the sea in line 4, and the metaphor describing the skylark's song as "unearthly minstrelsy" in line 24. However, there is a great deal of poetry in the imaginative adjectives used to describe landscape, particularly in the second section (lines 27–42). For example: "speckled", "shadowing", "o'er-browed", "faint", "cloud-like", "shoreless", etc.

This poem is classed as one of Coleridge's "Conversation Poems" because the style of the poem is conversational, as though Coleridge is speaking to a friend – indeed, it is as though the reader is his friend. This stance is created by the free flowing iambic pentameters in which the poem is written, the plain style, and by words and phrases such as "our" in line one, which supposes a "your", in other words, a listener; "I've said to my beloved", which is reported conversation as it would be phrased when speaking to another person.

The tone of the poem is intimate, conversational, but also exalted, especially at the end of section 1 and throughout section 2. In section 3, the tone is one of serious reasoning, though with touches of exaltation ("Praise it, O my Soul!). The poem ends on an exalted note with his wishes that all should enjoy such an "Abode" and will, when God's Kingdom comes.

THIS LIME-TREE BOWER MY PRISON

ADDRESSED TO CHARLES LAMB, OF THE INDIA HOUSE, LONDON

In the June of 1797 some long-expected friends paid a visit to the author's cottage; and on the morning of their arrival, he met with an accident, which disabled him from walking during the whole time of their stay. One evening, when they had left him for a few hours, he composed the following lines in the garden-bower.

Well, they are gone, and here must I remain,
This lime-tree bower my prison! I have lost
Beauties and feelings, such as would have been
Most sweet to my remembrance even when age
Had dimm'd mine eyes to blindness! They, meanwhile,   5
Friends, whom I never more may meet again,
On springy heath, along the hill-top edge,
Wander in gladness, and wind down, perchance,
To that still roaring dell, of which I told;
The roaring dell, o'erwooded, narrow, deep,   10
And only speckled by the mid-day sun;
Where its slim trunk the ash from rock to rock
Flings arching like a bridge;—that branchless ash,
Unsunn'd and damp, whose few poor yellow leaves
Ne'er tremble in the gale, yet tremble still,   15
Fann'd by the water-fall! and there my friends

Behold the dark green file of long lank weeds,
That all at once (a most fantastic sight!)
Still nod and drip beneath the dripping edge
Of the blue clay-stone.

        Now, my friends emerge   20
Beneath the wide wide Heaven—and view again
The many-steepled tract magnificent
Of hilly fields and meadows, and the sea,
With some fair bark, perhaps, whose sails light up
The slip of smooth clear blue betwixt two Isles   25
Of purple shadow! Yes! they wander on
In gladness all; but thou, methinks, most glad,
My gentle-hearted Charles! for thou hast pined
And hunger'd after Nature, many a year,
In the great City pent, winning thy way   30
With sad yet patient soul, through evil and pain
And strange calamity! Ah! slowly sink
Behind the western ridge, thou glorious Sun!
Shine in the slant beams of the sinking orb,
Ye purple heath-flowers! richlier burn, ye clouds!   35
Live in the yellow light, ye distant groves!
And kindle, thou blue Ocean! So my friend
Struck with deep joy may stand, as I have stood,
Silent with swimming sense; yea, gazing round
On the wide landscape, gaze till all doth seem   40
Less gross than bodily; and of such hues
As veil the Almighty Spirit, when yet he makes
Spirits perceive his presence.

          A delight
Comes sudden on my heart, and I am glad
As I myself were there! Nor in this bower,   45
This little lime-tree bower, have I not mark'd
Much that has sooth'd me. Pale beneath the blaze
Hung the transparent foliage; and I watch'd
Some broad and sunny leaf, and lov'd to see
The shadow of the leaf and stem above   50
Dappling its sunshine! And that walnut-tree
Was richly ting'd, and a deep radiance lay

Full on the ancient ivy, which usurps
Those fronting elms, and now, with blackest mass
Makes their dark branches gleam a lighter hue   55
Through the late twilight: and though now the bat
Wheels silent by, and not a swallow twitters,
Yet still the solitary humble-bee
Sings in the bean-flower! Henceforth I shall know
That Nature ne'er deserts the wise and pure;   60
No plot so narrow, be but Nature there,
No waste so vacant, but may well employ
Each faculty of sense, and keep the heart
Awake to Love and Beauty! and sometimes
'Tis well to be bereft of promis'd good,   65
That we may lift the soul, and contemplate
With lively joy the joys we cannot share.
My gentle-hearted Charles! when the last rook
Beat its straight path along the dusky air
Homewards, I blest it! deeming its black wing   70
(Now a dim speck, now vanishing in light)
Had cross'd the mighty Orb's dilated glory,
While thou stood'st gazing; or, when all was still,
Flew creeking o'er thy head, and had a charm
For thee, my gentle-hearted Charles, to whom   75
No sound is dissonant which tells of Life.

(1797)

GLOSSARY

bower – a shelter made from boughs or vines.
springy – describes the sensation of walking on soft turf.
bark – barque, a type of sailing ship.
Charles – Charles Lamb.
pent – pent up.
ye – the old plural of 'you'.
thou – the old singular of 'you'.
creeking – creaking, describing the sound of the quill-feathers.

QUESTIONS

NOTE: before answering the questions, read the first paragraph of the commentary which explains the situation which inspired the poem.

To what extent is the title an oxymoron? What is the effect of this?

Coleridge follows his friends adventures in imagination, Make a list of the places he imagines.

What elements of the sublime can be found in Coleridge's descriptions in lines 5 to 43.

How does he imagine that Charles Lamb responds to the walk?

Examine the religious sentiments expressed in lines 35 to 43 and say to what extent they are Pantheistic.

What beauties of nature in his immediate surroundings console Coleridge for missing the walk (see lines 43 to 76)?

How is Nature personified in lines 61 to 64? To what extent is this Pantheistic?

What qualities of empathy does the poem convey? Which words and phrases express that feeling?

Choose two or three words to describe the tone of the poem and explain why you chose them.

COMMENTARY

Coleridge explained the situation which inspired the poem in a letter to Southey:

The title of the poem is the idea around which everything else is built, particularly its the apparent contradiction in the idea that such a beautiful place as a "lime-tree bower" could be a "prison". It is a "prison" because Coleridge's injured foot meant that he could not accompany his friends on their walk. Instead, he follows them in imagination. As he does so, he writes descriptions of nature that are among the best in Romantic poetry. It is nature in its pleasantly wild form, of the type that can be seen in the paintings of Salvator Rosa. There is a "roaring dell, o'erwooded, narrow, deep", rocks, a "water-fall", distant views of "hilly fields and meadows and the sea". These sights inspire "gladness" (the word is used twice, in line 8 and line 27, and "glad", also in line 27). The last word refers to the feelings of Charles Lamb as Coleridge expresses an idea frequently used by himself and Wordsworth, that city life is unpleasant, and nature is a welcome escape: "for thou hast pined/ And hungered after Nature, many a year in the great City pent..."

He goes on to describe the beauty of the setting sun (thus indicating that the day he had to spend alone is nearly over). He imagines Lamb standing where he has stood, watching the sun set over the ocean and experiencing the same sensation of being spiritually uplifted. It is as though he sees beyond matter to "perceive his presence". Again there is a Pantheistic quality to this description, though it is expressed in conventionally Christian terms.

The final section begins with a powerful expression of fellow-feeling and empathy: I am as glad/ As I myself were there!" This epitomises the empathy shown throughout the poem as he has traced his friends' walk in imagination. He goes on to describe the beauties of his "lime-tree bower" where he has found much to compensate him for missing the walk. The description is a masterly evocation of light and shade, moving on to a description of the sights and sounds of twilight.

In lines 59 to 67 these beauties inspire him to personify Nature in Panthesistic way. Nature has a godlike power to comfort, which is shown in the way that he has been compensated for the beautiful sights he missed on the walk. He goes on to say that Nature always keeps the heart "Awake to Love and Beauty".

These exalted feelings move him to bless the last rook as it flew home. The significance of the rook is that it is a very different bird to the ones usually described by poets. It is a scavenger which makes a harsh cawing sound. That Coleridge should bless such a bird shows how elevated his mood is. It is interesting to compare this with the moment in *The Ancient Mariner* where the mariner blesses the water snakes.

The style of the poem is like a conversation, as though Coleridge is addressing a nearby listener. Indeed, the reader is drawn into this role, as though he or she was in the lime-tree bower with Coleridge. The conversational style is helped by the free-flowing pentameters, and everyday language.

The tone of the poem ranges from resigned and philosophical to exalted and empathic.

KUBLA KHAN: OR, A VISION IN A DREAM. A FRAGMENT

In Xanadu did Kubla Khan
A stately pleasure-dome decree:
Where Alph, the sacred river, ran
Through caverns measureless to man
    Down to a sunless sea.   5
So twice five miles of fertile ground
With walls and towers were girdled round:
And there were gardens bright with sinuous rills,
Where blossomed many an incense-bearing tree;
And here were forests ancient as the hills,   10
Enfolding sunny spots of greenery.

But oh! that deep romantic chasm which slanted
Down the green hill athwart a cedarn cover!
A savage place! as holy and enchanted
As e'er beneath a waning moon was haunted   15
By woman wailing for her demon-lover!
And from this chasm, with ceaseless turmoil seething,
As if this earth in fast thick pants were breathing,
A mighty fountain momently was forced:
Amid whose swift half-intermitted burst   20
Huge fragments vaulted like rebounding hail,
Or chaffy grain beneath the thresher's flail:

And 'mid these dancing rocks at once and ever
It flung up momently the sacred river.
Five miles meandering with a mazy motion 25
Through wood and dale the sacred river ran,
Then reached the caverns measureless to man,
And sank in tumult to a lifeless ocean:
And 'mid this tumult Kubla heard from far
Ancestral voices prophesying war! 30
    The shadow of the dome of pleasure
    Floated midway on the waves;
    Where was heard the mingled measure
    From the fountain and the caves.
It was a miracle of rare device, 35
A sunny pleasure-dome with caves of ice!

    A damsel with a dulcimer
    In a vision once I saw:
    It was an Abyssinian maid,
    And on her dulcimer she played, 40
    Singing of Mount Abora.
    Could I revive within me
    Her symphony and song,
    To such a deep delight 'twould win me,
That with music loud and long, 45
I would build that dome in air,
That sunny dome! those caves of ice!
And all who heard should see them there,
And all should cry, Beware! Beware!
His flashing eyes, his floating hair! 50
Weave a circle round him thrice,
And close your eyes with holy dread,
For he on honey-dew hath fed,
And drunk the milk of Paradise.

(1798)

GLOSSARY

Kubla Khan – a Mongol ruler who reined from 1260 to 1294.
girdled – encircled.

sinuous – having many curves and turns.

cedarn cover - covered with cedar trees.

chaffy – ' chaff' (not 'chav') is the husks of the grain separated by winnowing or threshing.

mazy – like a maze.

dulcimer – a hammered zither.

Abyssinian - of Abyssinia, today called Ethiopia.

Mount Abora – today called Amba Geshen, located in the Amhara Region of modern Ethiopia.

QUESTIONS

NOTE: Some background detail is needed to understand the poem, so read Part 1 of the Commentary before attempting the questions.

Look at some images of The Royal Pavilion, Brighton, and its interior and discuss how it relates to the poem.

Make a list of words and phrases that are exotic and/or orientalist (check the dictionary definitions of these words first).

Check the definitions of the 'sublime' and 'gothic', and look for examples in the poem.

Read the description in the commentary about how the composition of the poem was interrupted, and say where you think the interruption came.

How close is the opening of the poem to the lines Coleridge had been reading from *Purchas's Pilgrimage*? (see pages 25–26)

Which lines express Coleridge's regret for the part of the poem he had forgotten?

Some commentators think that the story of the person from Porlock was just an excuse because Coleridge got stuck in the middle of his poem (see p. 25). What do you think?

Who is the person described in the last 7 lines of the poem, and what is the "honey-dew" and "milk of paradise"?

COMMENTARY (PART 1)

This poem is often printed with the following note by Coleridge:

In the summer of the year 1797, the Author, then in ill health, had retired to a lonely farm-house between Porlock and Linton, on the Exmoor confines of Somerset and Devonshire. In consequence of a slight indisposition, an anodyne had been prescribed, from the effects of which he fell asleep in his chair at the moment that he was reading the following sentence, or words of the same substance, in 'Purchas's Pilgrimage': 'Here the Khan Kubla commanded a palace to be built, and a stately garden thereunto. And thus ten miles of fertile ground were inclosed with a wall.' The Author continued for about three hours in a profound sleep, at least of the external senses, during which time he has the most vivid confidence, that he could not have composed less than from two to three hundred lines; if that indeed can be called composition in which all the images rose up before him as *things*, with a parallel production of the correspondent expressions, without any sensation or consciousness of effort .On awaking he appeared to himself to have a distinct recollection of the whole, and taking his pen, ink, and paper, instantly and eagerly wrote down the lines that are here preserved. At this moment he was unfortunately called out by a person on business from Porlock, and detained by him above an hour, and on his return to his room, found, to his no small surprise and mortification, that though he still retained some vague and dim recollection of the general purport of the vision, yet, with the exception of some eight or ten scattered lines and images, all the rest had passed away like the images on the surface of a stream into which a stone has been cast, but, alas! without the after restoration of the latter!

The "anodyne" (a painkilling drug) was "two grains of Opium taken to check a dysentry" (Coleridge's own words from a different source). That, and other occasions of medial use, was probably the beginning of Coleridge's opium addiction.

Coleridge's opium addiction was real enough, but some

commentators (e.g., Elisabeth Schneider and the poet, Stevie Smith) believe that the story of the person from Porlock was made up as an excuse because he got stuck in the middle of the poem.

Xanadu is present day Zhenglan, which is to the northeast of Beijing. It was the summer capital of the Mongol ruler Kublai Khan, who reined from 1260 to 1294.

Coleridge got his information from *Purchas's Pilgrimes* (1625), which mentions Cublai Can and his palace at Xandu. This text has a more extensive description of the site. It is described (p. 80) as:

> A marvellous and artificial Palace of Marble and other stones ... He included sixteen miles within the circuit of the wall ... In this inclosure or Parke are goodly Meadowes, springs, rivers, red and fallow Deere, Fawnes carried thither for the Hawkes ... In the middest in a faire Wood hee hath built a royall House on pillars gilded and varnished, on every of which is a Dragon all gilt, which windeth his tayle about the pillar, with his head bearing up the loft, as also with his wings displayed on both sides; the cover also is of Reeds gilt and varnished ... The house itself may be sundred, and taken downe like a Tent and erected again. For it is sustained, when it is set up, with two hundred silken cords.

The description of the palace is vivid, and provides a visual context for how Coleridge imagines the palace of Xanadu.

An important element in the romantic movement was orientalism. It's beginnings can be traced to a general love of exotica in the 18th century. Artistic treatment of Eastern subjects took the form of furniture and interior decoration, using motifs from oriental art (particularly Chinese art), fabrics and pottery. The ultimate expression of Orientalist taste is the Royal Pavilion in Brighton (designed by John Nash, and begun in 1815). It can be appropriately described by a paraphrase of Coleridge's poem:

In Brighton did George, Prince of Wales
  A stately pleasure-dome decree.

Because that's what it was – a "pleasure dome", a summer palace for recreation only, designed and decorated in the latest style. *Kubla Khan* strikes exactly the same note of exotic orientalism 18 years before the Royal Pavilion was built.

Another important element in the romantic movement was the gothic (this is sometimes spelled as 'gothick' to distinguish the literary movement as opposed to the style of architecture). The gothic genre includes such motifs as: horror, fear, extreme emotions, the supernatural and romance.

A further element in the romantic movement was the sublime. This is a complex philosophical concept, but in its simplest form, it can be described as "overpowering, turbulent Nature inspiring heightened emotions" (adapted from Schopenhauer's definition).

COMMENTARY (PART 2)

NOTE: this part of the commentary gives information which answers some of the questions, so it is beast read after the students have attempted to answer the questions on page 24.

The place name and personal name in the first line immediately evoke the oriental exotic. Even without notes we understand that it refers to a Far Eastern city ruled by a dictatorial potentate (the word 'decree'' suggest his absolute power).

The "measureless caverns" have a hint of the sublime, and the "sunless sea" a hint of the gothic. The sublime is developed in the next stanza. It is a description of dramatic scenery which inspires emotion (Coleridge calls it "romantic"), the next two lines introduce a gothic element: it is "savage", "enchanted", and most extreme of all: "haunted by a woman wailing for her demon-lover!"

The elements of the sublime, particularly in the sense of "turbulent Nature" are further developed by the "ceaseless turmoil" of the "mighty fountain", and the "mazy motion" of the "sacred river".

The lines: "And 'mid this tumult Kubla heard from far/ Ancestral voices prophesying war!" suggest the introduction of narrative, as though the rest of the poem will be about the events of that war, which will be a "shadow of the dome of pleasure".

However, the development of the poem (introductory description, followed by the beginning of a narrative) breaks at this point. This is perhaps where the person from Porlock called, or where Coleridge got stuck (given his ability to narrate at length, seen in poems like *The Ancient Mariner*, and *Christabel*, the author is inclined towards the person from Porlock explanation).

Whether interrupted or stuck, Coleridge is clearly aware that the poem is not a complete poem, but (in the words of the full title, *A Fragment*). He rounds it off with the description of the "damsel with a dulcimer". The element of oriental exotic is continued, for she is an "Abyssinian maid", though now the orientalism is of the Middle Eastern variety – a switch which reinforces the discontinuity of the poem. Coleridge uses her to symbolise his muse. Her "symphony and song" is the poem he has forgotten. He says that if he could "revive" it he would "build that dome in air"; air, perhaps being a metaphor for imagination. However, it was left to the Prince Regent to built that dome in Brighton – a building which is almost the architectural equivalent of this poem. This shows, along with the elements of gothic and sublime, that Coleridge was deeply in touch with the *zeitgeist* (the spirit of his time), and that the person from Porlock is responsible for loss of what might have been one of the most powerful expressions of the romantic spirit.

The poem ends with a self-portrait of Coleridge as he might have been if he had finished the poem – something like an oriental shaman, who inspired exaggerated respect. The "honey-dew" and the "milk of Paradise" is, perhaps, the opium which inspired the lost masterpiece.

THE RIME OF THE ANCIENT MARINER (LITE)

This "lite" version of *The Ancient Mariner* is intended as an introduction to the study of a long and difficult poem. It is an abridged version with some stanzas omitted, and prose summaries linking the larger abridgements. Coleridge's prose glosses are given in simple modern English. The glossary is given "on the go" rather than at the end. The full text, with additional questions, is given in the next chapter.

PART I

An old sailor stops a young man who is going to a wedding feast.

It is an ancient Mariner,
And he stoppeth one of three.
'By thy long grey beard and glittering eye,
Now wherefore stopp'st thou me?

The Bridegroom's doors are opened wide,
And I am next of kin;
The guests are met, the feast is set:
May'st hear the merry **din**.'   *noise*

He holds him with his skinny hand,
'There was a ship,' **quoth** he.   *said*
'Hold off! unhand me, grey-beard **loon**!'   *lunatic*
Eftsoons his hand dropt he.   *soon*

29

He holds him with his glittering eye—
The Wedding-Guest stood still,
And listens like a three years' child:
The Mariner hath his will.

The Wedding-Guest sat on a stone:
He cannot choose but hear;
And thus **spake** on that ancient man,
The bright-eyed Mariner.

'The ship was cheered, the harbour cleared,
Merrily did we drop
Below the **kirk**, below the hill,
Below the lighthouse top.

The Sun came up upon the left,
Out of the sea came he!
And he shone bright, and on the right
Went down into the sea.

And now the STORM-BLAST came, and he
Was tyrannous and strong:
He struck with his o'ertaking wings,
And chased us south along.

With sloping masts and dipping prow,
As who pursued with yell and blow
Still treads the shadow of his foe,
And forward bends his head,
The ship drove fast, loud roared the blast,
And southward **aye** we fled.

And now there came both mist and snow,
And it grew wondrous cold:
And ice, mast-high, came floating by,
As green as emerald.

The ice was here, the ice was there,
The ice was all around:
It cracked and growled, and roared and

howled,
Like noises in a **swound**!   *swoon*

A sea-bird
came
through the
fog and was
welcomed
with great
joy.

At length did cross an Albatross,
Thorough the fog it came;
As if it had been a Christian soul,
We hailed it in God's name.

It ate the food it ne'er had eat,
And round and round it flew.
The ice did split with a thunder-fit;
The helmsman steered us through!

The
albatross is
seen as a
good omen
as it follows
the ship to
the north.

And a good south wind sprung up behind;
The Albatross did follow,
And every day, for food or play,
Came to the mariner's **hollo**!   *shout*

The old
sailor kills
the bird of
good omen.

'God save thee, ancient Mariner!
From the fiends, that plague thee thus!–
Why look'st thou so?'–With my cross-bow
I shot the ALBATROSS.

PART II

The Sun now rose upon the right:
Out of the sea came he,
Still hid in mist, and on the left
Went down into the sea.

And the good south wind still blew behind,
But no sweet bird did follow,
Nor any day for food or play
Came to the mariner's hollo!

The crew
criticise the
old sailor
for killing
the lucky
bird.

And I had done a hellish thing,
And it would work 'em woe:
For all **averred**, I had killed the bird   *asserted*
That made the breeze to blow.
Ah wretch! said they, the bird to slay,
That made the breeze to blow!

<table>
<tr>
<td width="20%">

When the fog clears they say he was right to do it, and thus make themselves accomplices to the crime.

</td>
<td width="60%">

Nor dim nor red, like God's own head,
The glorious Sun **uprist**:
Then all averred, I had killed the bird
That brought the fog and mist.
'Twas right, said they, such birds to slay,
That bring the fog and mist.

</td>
<td width="20%">

rose

</td>
</tr>
<tr>
<td>

The ship is suddenly becalmed.

</td>
<td>

Down dropt the breeze, the sails dropt
   down,
'Twas sad as sad could be;
And we did speak only to break
The silence of the sea!

Day after day, day after day,
We stuck, nor breath nor motion;
As idle as a painted ship
Upon a painted ocean.

</td>
<td></td>
</tr>
<tr>
<td>

And the Albatross begins to be revenged.

</td>
<td>

Water, water, every where,
And all the boards did shrink;
Water, water, every where,
Nor any drop to drink.

The very deep did rot: O Christ!
That ever this should be!
Yea, slimy things did crawl with legs
Upon the slimy sea.

About, about, in reel and rout
The death-fires danced at night;
The water, like a witch's oils,
Burnt green, and blue and white.

And every tongue, through utter drought,
Was withered at the root;
We could not speak, no more than if
We had been choked with soot.

</td>
<td></td>
</tr>
<tr>
<td>

The crew

</td>
<td>

Ah! well a-day! what evil looks

</td>
<td></td>
</tr>
</table>

throw all
the blame
on the old
sailor.

Had I from old and young!
Instead of the cross, the Albatross
About my neck was hung.

PART III

The Ancient Mariner sees a ship, but has to bite his arm and suck the blood to enable him to shout "A sail!" The joy of the crew turns to horror when they see that it is manned by a Spectre-Woman (called Life-in-Death) with Death as her mate (assistant). Life-in-Death and Death are casting lots for the ship's crew and Life-in-Death wins. Each crew member curses the ancient Mariner, then drops dead. Their souls fly past him "like the whizz of my cross-bow".

PART IV

The
wedding-
guest fears
that he is
talking to a
ghost;

'I fear thee, ancient Mariner!
I fear thy skinny hand!
And thou art long, and **lank**, and brown,   *thin*
As is the ribbed sea-sand.

but the old
sailor
assures him
that he did
not die.

I fear thee and thy glittering eye,
And thy skinny hand, so brown.'–
Fear not, fear not, thou Wedding-Guest!
This body dropt not down.

He tells him
about his
horrible
penance.

Alone, alone, all, all alone,
Alone on a wide wide sea!
And never a saint took pity on
My soul in agony.

He is sorry
that he, and
the slimy
things
should live
while so
many have
died.

The many men, so beautiful!
And they all dead did lie:
And a thousand thousand slimy things
Lived on; and so did I.
I looked upon the rotting sea,
And drew my eyes away;
I looked upon the rotting deck,
And there the dead men lay.

I looked to heaven, and tried to pray;
But or ever a prayer had **gusht**,   *gushed*
A wicked whisper came, and made
My heart as dry as dust.

I closed my lids, and kept them close,
And the balls like pulses beat;
For the sky and the sea, and the sea and
    the sky
Lay dead like a load on my weary eye,
And the dead were at my feet.

By the light
of the moon
he watches
the sea
creatures.

Beyond the shadow of the ship,
I watched the water-snakes:
They moved in tracks of shining white,
And when they reared, the elfish light
Fell off in **hoary** flakes.   *greyish-white*

Within the shadow of the ship
I watched their rich attire:
Blue, glossy green, and velvet black,
They coiled and swam; and every track
Was a flash of golden fire.

He is
impressed
by their
beauty and
happiness,
and
unknowingl
y blesses
them. The
spell begins
to break.

O happy living things! no tongue
Their beauty might declare:
A spring of love gushed from my heart,
And I blessed them unaware:
Sure my kind saint took pity on me,
And I blessed them unaware.
The self-same moment I could pray;
And from my neck so free
The Albatross fell off, and sank
Like lead into the sea.

PART V

The ancient Mariner falls asleep. While he is asleep it rains. Soon after, wind fills the sails. The bodies of the crew are filled by angelic spirits and they work the ship as before. At dawn, the spirits leave the bodies, but the ship sails on. The Spirit of the South Pole is under the keel of the ship and still wants revenge. The Mariner falls down in a faint, and hears two spirit voices saying that he will have to do more penance.

PART VI

The two spirits continued their discussion, then fly away. The Mariner awakes to see the crew standing on the deck glaring at him. Their curse has not gone away - that is his further penance. That curse is finally broken and a sweet breeze takes the ship back to his own country where he recognises a light-house, a hill and a church. The bodies of the crew are lying flat again and a "seraph-man" is standing on each corpse. Then he hears a "dash of oars". It is the Pilot and Pilot's boy, come to take him into the harbour. There is also a third person - a hermit. The mariner is happy to see him because: "He'll shrieve my soul, he'll wash away/ The Albatross's blood." (**shrieve** - give forgiveness for sins).

PART VII

The hermit of the wood.

This Hermit good lives in that wood
Which slopes down to the sea.
How loudly his sweet voice he rears!
He loves to talk with marineres
That come from a far countree.

The skiff-boat neared: I heard them talk,
'Why, this is strange, I **trow**!　　　　*believe*
Where are those lights so many and fair,
That signal made but now?'

As the boat approaches the ship the Hermit express his wonder at what he sees.

'Strange, by my faith!' the Hermit said—
'And they answered not our cheer!
The planks looked warped! and see those
　　　　sails,
How thin they are and sere!
I never saw aught like to them,　　　　*by*
Unless **perchance** it were　　　　*chance*

Brown skeletons of leaves that lag

My forest-brook along;
When the **ivy-tod** is heavy with snow,   *clump of*
And the owlet whoops to the wolf below,   *ivy*
That eats the she-wolf's young.'

'Dear Lord! it hath a fiendish look—
(The Pilot made reply)
I am a-feared'—'Push on, push on!'
Said the Hermit cheerily.

The boat came closer to the ship,
But I nor **spake** nor stirred;   *spoke*
The boat came close beneath the ship,
And straight a sound was heard.
Under the water it rumbled on,
The ship Still louder and more dread:
suddenly It reached the ship, it split the bay;
sinks. The ship went down like lead.

Stunned by that loud and dreadful sound,
Which sky and ocean **smote**,   *hit*
Like one that hath been seven days drowned
The old sailor My body lay afloat;
is saved in the But swift as dreams, myself I found
Pilot's boat. Within the Pilot's boat.

I took the oars: the Pilot's boy,
Who now doth crazy go,
Laughed loud and long, and all the while
His eyes went to and fro.
'Ha! ha!' **quoth** he, 'full plain I see,
The Devil knows how to row.'

And now, all in my own countree,
I stood on the firm land!
The Hermit stepped forth from the boat,
And scarcely he could stand.

'O shrieve me, shrieve me, holy man!'
The Hermit crossed his brow.

'Say quick,' quoth he, 'I bid thee say—
What manner of man art thou?'

Forthwith this frame of mine was wrenched
With a **woful** agony, *sad*
Which forced me to begin my tale;
And then it left me free.

Since then, at an uncertain hour,
That agony returns:
And till my ghastly tale is told,
This heart within me burns.

I pass, like night, from land to land;
I have strange power of speech;
That moment that his face I see,
I know the man that must hear me:
To him my tale I **teach**. *tell*

What loud uproar bursts from that door!
The wedding-guests are there:
But in the garden-bower the bride
And bride-maids singing are:
And hark the little vesper bell,
Which **biddeth** me to prayer! *tells*

O Wedding-Guest! this soul hath been
Alone on a wide wide sea:
So lonely 'twas, that God himself
Scarce seemèd there to be.

Farewell, farewell! but this I tell
To thee, thou Wedding-Guest!
He prayeth well, who loveth well
Both man and bird and beast.

He prayeth best, who loveth best
All things both great and small;
For the dear God who loveth us,
He made and loveth all.
The Mariner, whose eye is bright,

loves.
        Whose beard with age is hoar,
Is gone: and now the Wedding-Guest
Turned from the bridegroom's door.

He went like one that hath been stunned,
And is of sense forlorn:
A sadder and a wiser man,
He rose the morrow morn.

KEY EVENTS IN PART I:

- The story is told by an ancient Mariner (old sailor) to a wedding guest.

- They set off with a fair wind, but a storm drives the towards the south pole.

- An Albatross, a large sea-bird, appears, the ice breaks and a south wind drives the ship northwards.

- The ancient Mariner shoots the alabatross with his crossbow.

QUESTIONS ON PART I

The poem is written in ballad form used flexibly. Ballad form is a four-line stanza rhymed a b c b with 4 stresses in the first line, 3 in the second, 4 in the third and 3 in the fourth. Find an example of a "standard" stanza, underline the stressed syllables and the rhyming words.

Find an example of a non-standard stanza, i.e., with more lines, and/or with lines with internal rhyme. Underline the stressed syllables and rhyme.

Why is ballad form so appropriate for this story?

Archaic words are words that are no longer in use. List six examples, then comment on their effect.
What words and phrases are used to describe the ancient

Mariner?

What is it that puts the wedding guest in his power and compels him to listen?

What words and phrases does Coleridge use to describe the arctic? Explain how he uses personification in this description and what effect it has.

Compared to the long passages of description, what is the effect of the terse statement "I shot the ALBATROSS"?

KEY EVENTS IN PART II:

- The crew blame the ancient Mariner for killing the bird.

- When the fog clears, the crew say that it was right to kill the bird because it brought the fog, and by doing so they make themselves accomplices to the crime.

- The ship is suddenly becalmed and the albatross begins to be revenged.

- The crew throw all the blame on the old sailor.

QUESTIONS ON PART II

List six more examples of archaic words, then comment on their effect.

How do the other sailors become complicit in the ancient Mariner's crime?

What powerful image does Coleridge use to describe the becalmed ship?

How is repetition used to emphasise the lack of drinking water?

How does Coleridge describe the nightmarish quality of that "painted ocean"?

What powerful art imagery does he use? Why is it so powerful?

What image does he used to describe their thirst?

What contrast is presented in the last two lines?

KEY EVENTS IN PART III

- The Ancient Mariner sees a ship, but has to bite his arm and suck the blood to enable him to shout "A sail!"

- The joy of the crew turns to horror when they see that it is manned by a Spectre-Woman (called Life-in-Death) with Death as her mate (first officer).

- Life-in-Death and Death are casting lots for the ship's crew and Life-in-Death wins.

- Each crew member curses the ancient Mariner, then drops dead. Their souls fly past him "like the whizz of my cross-bow".

QUESTIONS ON PART III

Comment on the effectiveness of the cross-bow simile.

KEY EVENTS IN PART IV

- The wedding guest expresses his fear of the ancient Mariner because he thinks he is talking to a ghost.

- The Mariner is deeply sorry that all the men are dead while he and the "slimy things" live on.

- He tries to pray, but can't.

- He watches the sea creatures and is impressed by their beauty and happiness, and unknowingly blesses them.

- As a result, the curse begins to break.

QUESTIONS ON PART IV

How does the response of the wedding guest build up the sense of fear and horror in this part of the poem?

How does the description of the ancient Mariner add to this? What figures of speech are used to describe him?

What is the first unselfish thought that the Mariner has?

Comment on the effect of the simile that is used to describe his attempt to pray.

He now sees the "slimy things" in a different way. What words, phrases and figures of speech are used to describe them?

What does the Mariner do that begins to break the curse?

KEY EVENTS IN PART V

- The ancient Mariner falls asleep. While he is asleep it rains. Soon after, wind fills the sails.

- The bodies of the crew are filled by angelic spirits and they work the ship as before.

- At dawn, the spirits leave the bodies, but the ship sails on.

- The Spirit of the South Pole is under the keel of the ship and still wants revenge.

- The Mariner falls down in a faint, and hears two spirit voices saying that he will have to do more penance.

KEY EVENTS IN PART VI

The two spirits continued their discussion, then fly away.

The Mariner awakes to see the crew standing on the deck glaring at him. Their curse has not gone away – that is his further penance.

That curse is finally broken and a sweet breeze takes the ship back to his own country where he recognises a light-house, a hill and a church.

The bodies of the crew are lying flat again and a "seraph-man" is standing on each corpse.

Then he hears a "dash of oars". It is the Pilot and Pilot's boy, come to take him into the harbour.

There is also a third person – a hermit. The Mariner is happy to see him because: "He'll shrieve my soul, he'll wash away/ The Albatross's blood."

QUESTIONS ON PARTS V AND VI

What further revenge is taken by the Spirit of the South Pole?

How does the Mariner recognise his home?
Why is he so happy to see the hermit?

KEY EVENTS IN PART VII

- The Hermit is described.

- The Pilot says he is afraid, but the Hermit urges him to go on. Then the ship suddenly sinks.

- The Mariner is saved in the Pilot's boat.

- He begs the Hermit to hear his confession and give

forgiveness.

- Ever since, the Mariner has felt obliged to travel from country to country to tell his tale, and to teach, by his own example, love and reverence for all things that God made.

QUESTIONS ON PART VII

What things about the ship surprise the Hermit?

Comment on the extended simile that is used to describe the skeletons – what is the effect of extending it for a whole stanza?

What compulsion is affecting the Mariner?

The moral of the poem is given quite clearly in two lines in this section. Which lines are they? Restate the moral in your own words.

How well does the story fit the moral?

How does the ancient Mariner's story affect the wedding guest? How does it affect you? Is the moral still relevant to the modern age?

Further questions, many of a more general nature, can be found after the full version in the next chapter.

COMMENTARY

The Rime of the Ancient Mariner was published in 1798 in *Lyrical Ballads*, a joint publication by Coleridge and his friend William Wordsworth. It is the first poem in the book, though the 1789 version is slightly different from version that is usually read today. The main differences, apart from numerous minor changes to the text, are that there was more archaic spelling (for example, the title was given as *The Rime of the Ancyent Marinere*, and no marginal glosses (which were added in the 1817 edition).

The *Preface to the Lyrical Ballads* (added in 1800) expresses Wordsworth's theories about poetry, one of which was that poetry should be written in "a selection of the real language of men in a state of vivid sensation". *The Ancient Mariner*, of course, is a direct contradiction of this, being deliberately written in archaic language. There were several criticisms of this, most notably by Wordsworth, who wrote in a letter: "From what I can gather it seems that *The Ancient Mariner* has upon the whole been an injury to the volume, I mean that the old words and the strangeness of it have deterred readers from going on." However, though the poem did not fit Wordsworth's theory about poetic language, it caught the spirit of the Romantic movement, an important aspect of which was the gothic. Gothic literature includes such motifs as: horror, fear, extreme emotions, the supernatural and romance. It was particularly popular in the novel, a contemporary example being Radcliffe's *The Mysteries of Udolpho* (1794). It was also an influence on architecture, prime examples being Horace Walpole's Strawberry Hill (1749), Ashridge Park, by James Wyatt (1806), and Westminster Palace, by Sir Charles Barry and A.W. Pugin (1834).

The poem begins with a dramatic opening: the old sailor stopping the wedding guest with his "skinny hand". The reader immediately recognises the rhyme and metre of ballad form, and the archaic language. Ballad form is appropriate to a sailor's yarn (there are many traditional ballads of the sea). The archaic language also suggests these traditional ballads, and gives the impression that the story is an old one. The Mariner, without any introduction, begins his story. Coleridge builds a description of the Mariner with telling details: "skinny hand", "grey-beard loon", "glittering eye", "ancient". He describes the storm vividly by using personification. He storm is a "he", is "tyrannous" and "chased" the ship. The ice of the south seas is also vividly described with the similes "mast-high", and "green as emerald". The ice is personified: "It cracked and growled, and roared and howled". The Mariner then describes the coming of the Albatross and the good luck it brought: "the ice did split... the helmsman steered us through." Compared with all this vivid and lengthy description, the last line of this part is terse, which gives additional force to its shocking meaning.

Part II focuses on the consequences of killing the Albatross. The Mariner realises that he has done "a hellish thing". The world "hellish" places the act in a Christian context; it is a sin - though it is interesting to note that the sailor's beliefs about lucky and unlucky birds are superstition of the kind that is often criticised in the Bible. When the sun comes up, dispersing the mist, the rest of the crew agree with his act, saying it is right to kill birds "that bring the fog and mist". This is important to the moral dimension of the story, as it means that the rest of the crew, to some extent, share the Mariner's guilt. It is interesting how the phrase "all averred, I had killed the bird" is used, first to blame the Mariner, then later, to praise him. It emphasises that it is the same act, but the consequences are judged very differently. Vivid imagery is used to describe how the ship is becalmed, the repetition of the simile "painted" emphasising how very still everything was. Repetition is used again when the word "water" is repeated four times to emphasise the sailors' thirst. This is so vividly expressed, that a version of these lines has become a well-known saying. The horror of that becalmed sea is expressed through the description of sea monsters, which are "slimy things", personified "death-fires" that dance, and picking up the painting metaphor again, the colour of the water "like witch's oils". The last stanza of the section is symbolic as his cross is removed from his neck and replaced by the Albatross. This emphasises that he has sacrificed the protection that a Christian can expect from God, and that he must, instead, bear the consequences of his evil deed.

Part III describes the appearance of a ghost ship piloted by Death-in-Life and Death who cast lots for the crew. Death-in-Life wins and the crew drop down dead. The part ends with a simile comparing the flight of the souls to the "whizz" or the Mariner's cross-bow — a highly appropriate image. This sets the scene for the dramatic opening of Part IV, as the wedding guest thinks that the Mariner also died and is a ghost. There is a note of gothic horror in the repetition of the word "fear", which is used five times in the first two stanzas, and the description of old sailor with the alliterative "long, and lank" and the simile comparing him to the "ribbed sea-sand", emphasising the sunburned colour of his body, which is so thin that his ribs are outlined. The Mariner describes how his attempt to pray failed with a telling adjective and a vivid simile "A wicked whisper came, and made/ My heart as dry as dust." He watches the sea creatures for a while, and begins to appreciate their beauty, which is conveyed through many adjectives:

"Blue, glossy green, and velvet black" and a comparison of their tracks to "golden fire". He sees that they are "happy" and are "living things" of "beauty", and this feeling brings about the turning point (peripeteia) in the poem, where he feels "love", emphasises by the metaphor, "spring of love", extended with the word "gushed", and, in keeping with the Christian context of the poem, "blessed them". To symbolise the effect of this, the Albatross falls off his neck.

Part V is perhaps the least successful part of the poem. The ending of part IV led us to believe that the Mariner had learned his lesson and that the curse was ended, however, the Spirit of the South Pole wants further vengeance. This is discussed by two other spirits in the hearing of the Mariner. In Part VI, the crew awake and glare at him again, and then, for no clear reason, the curse finally ends and a fair breeze blows the ship home.

In Part VII, we see the ship from the point of view of a Hermit, who sails to it with the Pilot and his son. There is an extended image in which he compares the warped planks of the ship to "Brown skeletons of leaves" in winter. The extension of the image is full of gothic horror, the sound of the owlet's "whoops", and the wolf eating his young. That sense of horror is appropriate to the ship he is about to board. As soon as they get to the land, the Mariner is eager for the final step of his redemption. The curse was broken when he blessed the sea creatures but he still needs to be shriven (**shrive**: hear the confession of, assign penance to, and absolve). His penance is to wander from "land to land" telling his tale as an example. This leads into the moral of the poem, which is expressed in this stanza:

> He prayeth best, who loveth best
> All things both great and small;
> For the dear God who loveth us,
> He made and loveth all.

The last stanza of the poem is puzzling. The experience of meeting the Ancient mariner must have been stressful, to say the least, "harrowing" might be a better description, and, as a wedding guest, missed the ceremony, but the story has a positive moral. In which case, why should the wedding guest be "a sadder and a wiser man"? Perhaps it is because his experience has opened his eyes to the evil that is in the world and in man, though he, himself, managed to overcome it by learning to love "All things both great and small".

THE RIME OF THE ANCIENT MARINER
(FULL)

PART I

It is an ancient Mariner,
And he stoppeth one of three.
'By thy long grey beard and glittering eye,
Now wherefore stopp'st thou me?

The Bridegroom's doors are opened wide, 5
And I am next of kin;
The guests are met, the feast is set:
May'st hear the merry din.'

He holds him with his skinny hand,
'There was a ship,' quoth he. 10
'Hold off! unhand me, grey-beard loon!'
Eftsoons his hand dropt he.

He holds him with his glittering eye—
The Wedding-Guest stood still,
And listens like a three years' child: 15
The Mariner hath his will.

The Wedding-Guest sat on a stone:
He cannot choose but hear;

And thus spake on that ancient man,
The bright-eyed Mariner.   20

The Mariner tells how the ship sailed southward with a good wind and fair weather, till it reached the Line.

'The ship was cheered, the harbour cleared,
Merrily did we drop
Below the kirk, below the hill,
Below the lighthouse top.

The Sun came up upon the left,   25
Out of the sea came he!
And he shone bright, and on the right
Went down into the sea.

Higher and higher every day,
Till over the mast at noon—'   30
The Wedding-Guest here beat his breast,
For he heard the loud bassoon.

The Wedding-Guest heareth the bridal music; but the Mariner continueth his tale.

The bride hath paced into the hall,
Red as a rose is she;
Nodding their heads before her goes   35
The merry minstrelsy.

The Wedding-Guest he beat his breast,
Yet he cannot choose but hear;
And thus spake on that ancient man,
The bright-eyed Mariner.   40

The ship driven by a storm toward the south pole.

And now the STORM-BLAST came, and he
Was tyrannous and strong:
He struck with his o'ertaking wings,
And chased us south along.

With sloping masts and dipping prow,   45
As who pursued with yell and blow
Still treads the shadow of his foe,
And forward bends his head,
The ship drove fast, loud roared the blast,
And southward aye we fled.   50

And now there came both mist and snow,
And it grew wondrous cold:
And ice, mast-high, came floating by,
As green as emerald.

And through the drifts the snowy clifts   55
Did send a dismal sheen:
Nor shapes of men nor beasts we ken—
The ice was all between.

The ice was here, the ice was there,
The ice was all around: 60
It cracked and growled, and roared and
howled,
Like noises in a swound!

At length did cross an Albatross,
Thorough the fog it came;   65
As if it had been a Christian soul,
We hailed it in God's name.

It ate the food it ne'er had eat,
And round and round it flew.
The ice did split with a thunder-fit;
The helmsman steered us through!   70

And a good south wind sprung up behind;
The Albatross did follow,
And every day, for food or play,
Came to the mariner's hollo!

In mist or cloud, on mast or shroud,   75
It perched for vespers nine;
Whiles all the night, through fog-smoke white,
Glimmered the white Moon-shine.'

'God save thee, ancient Mariner!
From the fiends, that plague thee thus!—   80
Why look'st thou so?' — With my cross-bow
I shot the ALBATROSS.

PART II

The Sun now rose upon the right:
Out of the sea came he,
Still hid in mist, and on the left   85
Went down into the sea.

And the good south wind still blew behind,
But no sweet bird did follow,
Nor any day for food or play
Came to the mariner's hollo!   90

And I had done a hellish thing,
And it would work 'em woe:
For all averred, I had killed the bird
That made the breeze to blow.
Ah wretch! said they, the bird to slay,   95
That made the breeze to blow!

Nor dim nor red, like God's own head,
The glorious Sun uprist:
Then all averred, I had killed the bird
That brought the fog and mist.   100
'Twas right, said they, such birds to slay,
That bring the fog and mist.

The fair breeze blew, the white foam flew,
The furrow followed free;
We were the first that ever burst   105
Into that silent sea.

Down dropt the breeze, the sails dropt down,
'Twas sad as sad could be;
And we did speak only to break
The silence of the sea!   110

All in a hot and copper sky,
The bloody Sun, at noon,
Right up above the mast did stand,
No bigger than the Moon.

His shipmates cry out against the ancient Mariner, for killing the bird of good luck.

But when the fog cleared off, they justify the same, and thus make themselves accomplices in the crime.

The fair breeze continues; the ship enters the Pacific Ocean, and sails northward, even till it reaches the Line.

The ship hath been suddenly becalmed.

Day after day, day after day,   115
We stuck, nor breath nor motion;
As idle as a painted ship
Upon a painted ocean.

Water, water, every where,
And all the boards did shrink;   120
Water, water, every where,
Nor any drop to drink.

The very deep did rot: O Christ!
That ever this should be!
Yea, slimy things did crawl with legs   125
Upon the slimy sea.

About, about, in reel and rout
The death-fires danced at night;
The water, like a witch's oils,
Burnt green, and blue and white.   130

And some in dreams assurèd were
Of the Spirit that plagued us so;
Nine fathom deep he had followed us
From the land of mist and snow.

And every tongue, through utter drought,   135
Was withered at the root;
We could not speak, no more than if
We had been choked with soot.

Ah! well a-day! what evil looks
Had I from old and young!   140
Instead of the cross, the Albatross
About my neck was hung.

PART III

There passed a weary time. Each throat
Was parched, and glazed each eye.
A weary time! a weary time!   145
How glazed each weary eye,

And the Albatross begins to be avenged.

A Spirit had followed them; one of the invisible inhabitants of this planet, neither departed souls nor angels; concerning whom the learned Jew, Josephus, and the Platonic.

The shipmates, in their sore distress, would fain throw the whole guilt on the ancient Mariner: in sign whereof they hang the dead sea-bird round his neck.

The ancient Mariner beholdeth

a sign in the element afar off.

When looking westward, I beheld
A something in the sky.

At first it seemed a little speck,
And then it seemed a mist;
It moved and moved, and took at last   150
A certain shape, I wist.

A speck, a mist, a shape, I wist!
And still it neared and neared:
As if it dodged a water-sprite,
It plunged and tacked and veered.   155

At its nearer approach, it seemeth him to be a ship; and at a dear ransom he freeth his speech from the bonds of thirst.

With throats unslaked, with black lips baked,
We could nor laugh nor wail;
Through utter drought all dumb we stood!
I bit my arm, I sucked the blood,
And cried, A sail! a sail!   160

A flash of joy.

With throats unslaked, with black lips baked,
Agape they heard me call:
Gramercy! they for joy did grin,
And all at once their breath drew in.   165
As they were drinking all.

And horror follows. For can it be a ship that comes onward without wind or tide?

See! see! (I cried) she tacks no more!
Hither to work us weal;
Without a breeze, without a tide,
She steadies with upright keel!   170

The western wave was all a-flame.
The day was well nigh done!
Almost upon the western wave
Rested the broad bright Sun;
When that strange shape drove suddenly   175

It seemeth him but the skeleton of a ship.

Betwixt us and the Sun.

And straight the Sun was flecked with bars,
(Heaven's Mother send us grace!)
As if through a dungeon-grate he peered

And its ribs are seen as bars on the face of the setting Sun.

With broad and burning face.   180

Alas! (thought I, and my heart beat loud)
How fast she nears and nears!
Are those her sails that glance in the Sun,
Like restless gossameres?

The Spectre-Woman and her Death-mate, and no other on board the skeleton ship.

Are those *her* ribs through which the Sun   185
Did peer, as through a grate?
And is that Woman all her crew?
Is that a DEATH? and are there two?
Is DEATH that woman's mate?

Like vessel, like crew!

Her lips were red, *her* looks were free,   190
Her locks were yellow as gold:
Her skin was as white as leprosy,
The Night-mare LIFE-IN-DEATH was she,
Who thicks man's blood with cold.

Death and Life-in-Death have diced for the ship's crew, and she (the latter) winneth the ancient Mariner.

The naked hulk alongside came,   195
And the twain were casting dice;
'The game is done! I've won! I've won!'
Quoth she, and whistles thrice.

No twilight within the courts of the Sun.

The Sun's rim dips; the stars rush out;
At one stride comes the dark;   200
With far-heard whisper, o'er the sea,
Off shot the spectre-bark.

At the rising of the Moon,

We listened and looked sideways up!
Fear at my heart, as at a cup,
My life-blood seemed to sip!   205
The stars were dim, and thick the night,
The steersman's face by his lamp gleamed
    white;
From the sails the dew did drip—
Till clomb above the eastern bar

One after another,

The hornèd Moon, with one bright star   210
Within the nether tip.

One after one, by the star-dogged Moon,
Too quick for groan or sigh,
Each turned his face with a ghastly pang,
And cursed me with his eye.   215

Four times fifty living men,
(And I heard nor sigh nor groan)
With heavy thump, a lifeless lump,
They dropped down one by one.

The souls did from their bodies fly,—   220
They fled to bliss or woe!
And every soul, it passed me by,
Like the whizz of my cross-bow!

PART IV

'I fear thee, ancient Mariner!
I fear thy skinny hand!   225
And thou art long, and lank, and brown,
As is the ribbed sea-sand.

I fear thee and thy glittering eye,
And thy skinny hand, so brown.'—
Fear not, fear not, thou Wedding-Guest!   230
This body dropt not down.

Alone, alone, all, all alone,
Alone on a wide wide sea!
And never a saint took pity on
My soul in agony.   235

The many men, so beautiful!
And they all dead did lie:
And a thousand thousand slimy things
Lived on; and so did I.

I looked upon the rotting sea,   240
And drew my eyes away;
I looked upon the rotting deck,
And there the dead men lay.

His shipmates drop down dead.

But Life-in-Death begins her work on the ancient Mariner.

The Wedding-Guest feareth that a Spirit is talking to him;

But the ancient Mariner assureth him of his bodily life, and proceedeth to relate his horrible penance.

He despiseth the creatures of the calm,

And envieth that they should live, and so many lie dead.

I looked to heaven, and tried to pray;
But or ever a prayer had gusht,   245
A wicked whisper came, and made
My heart as dry as dust.

I closed my lids, and kept them close,
And the balls like pulses beat;
For the sky and the sea, and the sea and the sky   250
Lay dead like a load on my weary eye,
And the dead were at my feet.

But the curse liveth for him in the eye of the dead men.

The cold sweat melted from their limbs,
Nor rot nor reek did they:
The look with which they looked on me   255
Had never passed away.

In his loneliness and fixedness he yearneth towards the journeying Moon, and the stars that still sojourn, yet still move onward; and every where the blue sky belongs to them, and is their appointed rest, and their native country and their own natural homes, which they enter unannounced, as lords that are certainly expected and yet there is a silent joy at their arrival.

An orphan's curse would drag to hell
A spirit from on high;
But oh! more horrible than that
Is the curse in a dead man's eye!   260
Seven days, seven nights, I saw that curse,
And yet I could not die.

The moving Moon went up the sky,
And no where did abide:
Softly she was going up,   265
And a star or two beside–

By the light of the Moon he beholdeth God's creatures of the great calm.

Her beams bemocked the sultry main,
Like April hoar-frost spread;
But where the ship's huge shadow lay,
The charmèd water burnt alway   270
A still and awful red.

Beyond the shadow of the ship,
I watched the water-snakes:
They moved in tracks of shining white,
And when they reared, the elfish light   275
Fell off in hoary flakes.

Within the shadow of the ship
I watched their rich attire:
Blue, glossy green, and velvet black,
They coiled and swam; and every track
Was a flash of golden fire.

O happy living things! no tongue
Their beauty might declare:
A spring of love gushed from my heart,
And I blessed them unaware:
Sure my kind saint took pity on me,
And I blessed them unaware.

The self-same moment I could pray;
And from my neck so free
The Albatross fell off, and sank
Like lead into the sea.

PART V

Oh sleep! it is a gentle thing,
Beloved from pole to pole!
To Mary Queen the praise be given!
She sent the gentle sleep from Heaven,
That slid into my soul.

The silly buckets on the deck,
That had so long remained,
I dreamt that they were filled with dew;
And when I awoke, it rained.

My lips were wet, my throat was cold,
My garments all were dank;
Sure I had drunken in my dreams,
And still my body drank.

I moved, and could not feel my limbs:
I was so light—almost
I thought that I had died in sleep,
And was a blessed ghost.

Their beauty and their happiness.

He blesseth them in his heart.

The spell begins to break.

By grace of the holy Mother, the ancient Mariner is refreshed with rain.

He heareth sounds and seeth strange sights and commotions in the sky and the element.

And soon I heard a roaring wind:
It did not come anear;   310
But with its sound it shook the sails,
That were so thin and sere.

The upper air burst into life!
And a hundred fire-flags sheen,
To and fro they were hurried about!   315
And to and fro, and in and out,
The wan stars danced between.

And the coming wind did roar more loud,
And the sails did sigh like sedge,
And the rain poured down from one black
    cloud;   320
The Moon was at its edge.

The thick black cloud was cleft, and still
The Moon was at its side:
Like waters shot from some high crag,
The lightning fell with never a jag,   325
A river steep and wide.

The loud wind never reached the ship,
Yet now the ship moved on!
Beneath the lightning and the Moon
The dead men gave a groan.   330

They groaned, they stirred, they all uprose,
Nor spake, nor moved their eyes;
It had been strange, even in a dream,
To have seen those dead men rise.

The helmsman steered, the ship moved on;   335
Yet never a breeze up-blew;
The mariners all 'gan work the ropes,
Where they were wont to do;
They raised their limbs like lifeless tools—
We were a ghastly crew.   340

The bodies of the ship's crew are inspired, and the ship moves on;

The body of my brother's son
Stood by me, knee to knee:
The body and I pulled at one rope,
But he said nought to me.

'I fear thee, ancient Mariner!'   345
Be calm, thou Wedding-Guest!
'Twas not those souls that fled in pain,
Which to their corses came again,
But a troop of spirits blest:

For when it dawned—they dropped their arms, 350
And clustered round the mast;
Sweet sounds rose slowly through their
  mouths,
And from their bodies passed.

Around, around, flew each sweet sound,
Then darted to the Sun;   355
Slowly the sounds came back again,
Now mixed, now one by one.

Sometimes a-dropping from the sky
I heard the sky-lark sing;
Sometimes all little birds that are, 360
How they seemed to fill the sea and air
With their sweet jargoning!

And now 'twas like all instruments,
Now like a lonely flute;
And now it is an angel's song,   365
That makes the heavens be mute.

It ceased; yet still the sails made on
A pleasant noise till noon,
A noise like of a hidden brook
In the leafy month of June,   370
That to the sleeping woods all night
Singeth a quiet tune.

But not by the souls of the men, nor by dæmons of earth or middle air, but by a blessed troop of angelic spirits, sent down by the invocation of the guardian saint.

Till noon we quietly sailed on,
Yet never a breeze did breathe:
Slowly and smoothly went the ship,   375
Moved onward from beneath.

Under the keel nine fathom deep,
From the land of mist and snow,
The spirit slid: and it was he
That made the ship to go.   380
The sails at noon left off their tune,
And the ship stood still also.

The Sun, right up above the mast,
Had fixed her to the ocean:
But in a minute she 'gan stir,   385
With a short uneasy motion—
Backwards and forwards half her length
With a short uneasy motion.

Then like a pawing horse let go,
She made a sudden bound: 390
It flung the blood into my head,
And I fell down in a swound.

How long in that same fit I lay,
I have not to declare;
But ere my living life returned,   395
I heard and in my soul discerned
Two voices in the air.

'Is it he?' quoth one, 'Is this the man?
By him who died on cross,
With his cruel bow he laid full low   400
The harmless Albatross.

The spirit who bideth by himself
In the land of mist and snow,
He loved the bird that loved the man
Who shot him with his bow.'   405

The lonesome Spirit from the south-pole carries on the ship as far as the Line, in obedience to the angelic troop, but still requireth vengeance.

The Polar Spirit's fellow-dæmons, the invisible inhabitants of the element, take part in his wrong; and two of them relate, one to the other, that penance long and heavy for the ancient Mariner hath been accorded to the Polar Spirit, who returneth southward.

The other was a softer voice,
As soft as honey-dew:
Quoth he, 'The man hath penance done,
And penance more will do.'

PART VI

FIRST VOICE
'But tell me, tell me! speak again,   410
Thy soft response renewing—
What makes that ship drive on so fast?
What is the ocean doing?'

SECOND VOICE
Still as a slave before his lord,
The ocean hath no blast;   415
His great bright eye most silently
Up to the Moon is cast—

If he may know which way to go;
For she guides him smooth or grim.
See, brother, see! how graciously   420
She looketh down on him.'

FIRST VOICE
'But why drives on that ship so fast,
Without or wave or wind?'

SECOND VOICE
'The air is cut away before,
And closes from behind.   425

Fly, brother, fly! more high, more high!
Or we shall be belated:
For slow and slow that ship will go,
When the Mariner's trance is abated.'

I woke, and we were sailing on   430
As in a gentle weather:
'Twas night, calm night, the moon was high;

The dead men stood together.

All stood together on the deck,
For a charnel-dungeon fitter: 435
All fixed on me their stony eyes,
That in the Moon did glitter.

The pang, the curse, with which they died,
Had never passed away:
I could not draw my eyes from theirs,   440
Nor turn them up to pray.

And now this spell was snapt: once more
I viewed the ocean green,
And looked far forth, yet little saw
Of what had else been seen—   445

Like one, that on a lonesome road
Doth walk in fear and dread,
And having once turned round walks on,
And turns no more his head;
Because he knows, a frightful fiend   450
Doth close behind him tread.

But soon there breathed a wind on me,
Nor sound nor motion made:
Its path was not upon the sea,
In ripple or in shade.   455

It raised my hair, it fanned my cheek
Like a meadow-gale of spring—
It mingled strangely with my fears,
Yet it felt like a welcoming.

Swiftly, swiftly flew the ship,   460
Yet she sailed softly too:
Sweetly, sweetly blew the breeze—
On me alone it blew.

Oh! dream of joy! is this indeed

The light-house top I see? 465
Is this the hill? is this the kirk?
Is this mine own countree?

We drifted o'er the harbour-bar,
And I with sobs did pray—
O let me be awake, my God! 470
Or let me sleep alway.

The harbour-bay was clear as glass,
So smoothly it was strewn!
And on the bay the moonlight lay,
And the shadow of the Moon. 475

The rock shone bright, the kirk no less,
That stands above the rock:
The moonlight steeped in silentness
The steady weathercock.

And the bay was white with silent light, 480
Till rising from the same,
Full many shapes, that shadows were,
In crimson colours came.

A little distance from the prow
Those crimson shadows were: 485
I turned my eyes upon the deck—
Oh, Christ! what saw I there!

Each corse lay flat, lifeless and flat,
And, by the holy rood!
A man all light, a seraph-man, 490
On every corse there stood.

This seraph-band, each waved his hand:
It was a heavenly sight!
They stood as signals to the land,
Each one a lovely light; 495

This seraph-band, each waved his hand,

No voice did they impart—
No voice; but oh! the silence sank
Like music on my heart.

But soon I heard the dash of oars,   500
I heard the Pilot's cheer;
My head was turned perforce away
And I saw a boat appear.

The Pilot and the Pilot's boy,
I heard them coming fast:
Dear Lord in Heaven! it was a joy   505
The dead men could not blast.

I saw a third—I heard his voice:
It is the Hermit good!
He singeth loud his godly hymns   510
That he makes in the wood.
He'll shrieve my soul, he'll wash away
The Albatross's blood.

PART VII

This Hermit good lives in that wood
Which slopes down to the sea.   515
How loudly his sweet voice he rears!
He loves to talk with marineres
That come from a far countree.

He kneels at morn, and noon, and eve—
He hath a cushion plump: 540
It is the moss that wholly hides
The rotted old oak-stump.

The skiff-boat neared: I heard them talk,
'Why, this is strange, I trow!
Where are those lights so many and fair,   525
That signal made but now?'

'Strange, by my faith!' the Hermit said—
And they answered not our cheer!

The planks looked warped! and see those sails,
How thin they are and sere!　　　　　　　530
I never saw aught like to them,
Unless perchance it were

Brown skeletons of leaves that lag
My forest-brook along;
When the ivy-tod is heavy with snow,　　　535
And the owlet whoops to the wolf below,
That eats the she-wolf's young.'

'Dear Lord! it hath a fiendish look–
(The Pilot made reply)
I am a-feared'–'Push on, push on!'
Said the Hermit cheerily.　　　　　　　540

The boat came closer to the ship,
But I nor spake nor stirred;
The boat came close beneath the ship,
And straight a sound was heard.　　　　545

Under the water it rumbled on,
Still louder and more dread:
It reached the ship, it split the bay;
The ship went down like lead.

Stunned by that loud and dreadful sound,　550
Which sky and ocean smote,
Like one that hath been seven days drowned
My body lay afloat;
But swift as dreams, myself I found
Within the Pilot's boat.　　　　　　　555

Upon the whirl, where sank the ship,
The boat spun round and round;
And all was still, save that the hill
Was telling of the sound.

I moved my lips–the Pilot shrieked　　　560
And fell down in a fit;

The holy Hermit raised his eyes,
And prayed where he did sit.

I took the oars: the Pilot's boy,
Who now doth crazy go,   565
Laughed loud and long, and all the while
His eyes went to and fro.
'Ha! ha!' quoth he, 'full plain I see,
The Devil knows how to row.'

And now, all in my own countree,   570
I stood on the firm land!
The Hermit stepped forth from the boat,
And scarcely he could stand.

'O shrieve me, shrieve me, holy man!'
The Hermit crossed his brow.   575
'Say quick,' quoth he, 'I bid thee say—
What manner of man art thou?'

Forthwith this frame of mine was wrenched
With a woful agony,
Which forced me to begin my tale;   580
And then it left me free.

Since then, at an uncertain hour,
That agony returns:
And till my ghastly tale is told,
This heart within me burns.   585

I pass, like night, from land to land;
I have strange power of speech;
That moment that his face I see,
I know the man that must hear me:
To him my tale I teach.   590

What loud uproar bursts from that door!
The wedding-guests are there:
But in the garden-bower the bride
And bride-maids singing are:

And hark the little vesper bell,   595
Which biddeth me to prayer!

O Wedding-Guest! this soul hath been
Alone on a wide wide sea:
So lonely 'twas, that God himself
Scarce seemèd there to be.   600

O sweeter than the marriage-feast,
'Tis sweeter far to me,
To walk together to the kirk
With a goodly company!–

To walk together to the kirk,   605
And all together pray,
While each to his great Father bends,
Old men, and babes, and loving friends
And youths and maidens gay!

Farewell, farewell! but this I tell   610
To thee, thou Wedding-Guest!
He prayeth well, who loveth well
Both man and bird and beast.

He prayeth best, who loveth best
All things both great and small;   615
For the dear God who loveth us,
He made and loveth all.

The Mariner, whose eye is bright,
Whose beard with age is hoar,
Is gone: and now the Wedding-Guest   620
Turned from the bridegroom's door.

He went like one that hath been stunned,
And is of sense forlorn:
A sadder and a wiser man,
He rose the morrow morn.   625
    (1797-1798)

GLOSSARY

I wist – I knew.
gramercy – short for "God grant mercy!"
betwixt – between
spectre-bark – ghost ship. A **barque** is a type of sailing ship.
silly – here, 'blessed', from Anglo-Saxon 'gesælig'.
wan – pale and ill-looking.
sedge – a grass-like plant.
corses – corpses
charnel-dungeon – like a crypt, where the dead are entombed.
shrieve – shrive: hear confession, assign penance, and absolve.

QUESTIONS

Read the whole poem with a particular focus on the parts that were abridged in the "Lite" version, then work through the following questions, many of which concern the poem as a whole, and in the broader context of Romantic literature.

Read the translation of the epigraph on pages 70-71 and consider why it is a good introduction to this poem.

Wordsworth said that the "the principal person has no distinct character". However, his character is built up gradually through numerous descriptive touches throughout the poem, and his moral journey, in which he learns an important lesson. Write a detailed description of the character of the Ancient Mariner.

Why is the archaic language and use of ballad form appropriate to this story? Find and comment on some examples of archaic language in Parts III, V and VI. Analyse the verse from of two stanzas, one standard ballad form, the other irregular, from these parts.

A lot of personification is used in the poem. Give examples from any part, particularly Parts III, V and VI, and say why they are effective.

In what sense is the poem (in the words of Jerome McGann) a

salvation story?

In the *Preface to the Lyrical Ballads*, Wordsworth wrote about the importance of "vivid sensation". Give examples from this poem.

How accurate is it to classify this poem as gothic literature? (Gothic literature includes such motifs as: horror, fear, extreme emotions, the supernatural and romance.) give detailed examples to justify your answer.

Track Christian elements through the poem (e.g., confession and absolution, prayer, the Hermit, the Mariner's cross, the Seraphs) and compare and contrast them to superstitious elements (Death personified, Life-in -Death, lucky and unlucky birds, the Spectre-Bark, the Sprit of the South Pole). Do the superstitious elements undermine the Christian moral at the end of the poem?

Examine Coleridge's use of repetition in the poem. Find some examples and say what effect they have. Is it used more frequently at key moments in the poem?

Compare and contrast the language used to describe the sea creatures when they are first seen, and later, in Part III, when the Mariner sees them in a different way.

Re-read Part V, and discuss how effective it is. Does it detract from the clarity of the plot? Is it merely padding, or does it serve an important purpose?

In *Table Talk*, Coleridge tells us that the poem has been criticised for lacking a moral. There is a kind of moral in Part VII, but how successful is it? Does it arise naturally from the events in the story, or does it seem contrived?

Compare Coleridge's style with the example of 18th century verse that he and Wordsworth wanted to replace. (See pages 6-7).

How does this story explore the Christian concepts of penance and redemption?

There are many symbols in the poem, for example: Albatross,

ice, moon, sea-creatures, storm, the Mariner's cross, the wedding. Explore how these and other symbols are used in the poem.

Write a logbook of the Mariner's journey.

The story is dramatised by being told to a wedding guest. what does this add to the power of the narrative?

Allegory is a figure of speech in which abstract ideas and principles are described in terms of characters, figures, and events. The objective of its use is to teach some kind of a moral lesson. (literearydevices.net). How far is *The Ancient Mariner* an allegory?

ADDITIONAL COMMENTARY

This epigraph was published with poem (the text of the 1798 edition is slightly different, but the message is the same).

Facile credo, plures esse Naturas invisibiles quam visibiles in rerum universitate. Sed horum omnium familiam quis nobis enarrabit? et gradus et cognationes et discrimina et singulorum munera? Quid agunt? quae loca habitant? Harum rerum notitiam semper ambivit ingenium humanum, nunquam attigit. Juvat, interea, non diffiteor, quandoque in animo, tanquam in tabulâ, majoris et melioris mundi imaginem contemplari: ne mens assuefacta hodiernae vitae minutiis se contrahat nimis, et tota subsidat in pusillas cogitationes. Sed veritati interea invigilandum est, modusque servandus, ut certa ab incertis, diem a nocte, distinguamus.
—T. BURNET, *Archaeol. Phil.* p. 68.

TRANSLATION:

It is easy to believe that there are more invisible things than visible in the universe. But of these who shall tell us of all the family? degrees, connections and distinguishing features and functions? What they do? which dwell in the places? The human mind has always circled around a knowledge of these things, never attaining it. It helps, in the mean time, I do not deny, and sometimes in the heart, as in a picture of a larger and better world; to contemplate the image of these things, lest the mind, habituated to trivia of daily life, wholly sink into trifles. But be careful about the truth, and in the meantime, observe a certain distinction between uncertain, day and night.

This epigraph makes a good introduction to the poem because it prepares us to accept its supernatural elements. Burnet says that "there are more invisible things than visible in the universe", and this prepares the reader for Coleridge's large cast of supernatural beings which include Death-in-Life, The Spirit of the South Pole, the Seraph-Man, and many more.

CHRISTABEL (LITE)

Christabel is an unfinished poem in two parts. This 'lite' version consists of a short summary of each part, followed by an abridgement of the text, a glossary, study questions, and a commentary. When you have studied the "lite" version, go on to the full version in the next chapter, where you will find additional questions, referring to the whole poem, and further commentary.

SUMMARY OF PART I

Christabel is introduced "praying in the midnight wood," beneath a "huge oak-tree". She is startled by "moanings" and on the "other side of the oak" finds "a damsel bright" "in sore distress". Geraldine explains, rather suspiciously, how she came to be there, and Christabel takes her home to Langdale Hall, the castle of her father, Sir Leoline. The howling of "the mastiff bitch" and the attempt to banish the spirit of Christabel's dead mother are the first clues of Geraldine's supernatural character. The two women now go to bed together. As Geraldine disrobes her "bosom and half her side" is glimpsed, and there is something sinister about it, as it is followed by the line: "shield sweet Christabel!" For an hour Christabel, in "her arms", is "dreaming fearfully" — from which state of terror she is delivered by her guardian mother.

PART I

'Tis the middle of night by the castle clock,
And the owls have awakened the crowing cock;
Tu–whit!—Tu–whoo!
And hark, again! the crowing cock,
How drowsily it crew.
Sir Leoline, the Baron rich,
Hath a toothless mastiff bitch;
From her kennel beneath the rock
She maketh answer to the clock,
Four for the quarters, and twelve for the hour;
Ever and aye, by shine and shower,
Sixteen short howls, not over loud;
Some say, she sees my lady's shroud.

The lovely lady, Christabel,
Whom her father loves so well,
What makes her in the wood so late,
A furlong from the castle gate?
She had dreams all yesternight
Of her own betrothéd knight;
And she in the midnight wood will pray
For the weal of her lover that's far away.

She stole along, she nothing spoke,
The sighs she heaved were soft and low,
And naught was green upon the oak
But moss and rarest misletoe:
She kneels beneath the huge oak tree,
And in silence prayeth she.

The lady sprang up suddenly,
The lovely lady, Christabel!
It moaned as near, as near can be,
But what it is she cannot tell.–
On the other side it seems to be,
Of the huge, broad-breasted, old oak tree.

There she sees a damsel bright,

Drest in a silken robe of white,
That shadowy in the moonlight shone:
The neck that made that white robe wan,
Her stately neck, and arms were bare;
Her blue-veined feet unsandal'd were,
And wildly glittered here and there
The gems entangled in her hair.
I guess, 'twas frightful there to see
A lady so richly clad as she—
Beautiful exceedingly!

Mary mother, save me now!
(Said Christabel,) And who art thou?

The lady strange made answer meet,
And her voice was faint and sweet:—
Have pity on my sore distress,
I scarce can speak for weariness:
Stretch forth thy hand, and have no fear!
Said Christabel, How camest thou here?
And the lady, whose voice was faint and sweet,
Did thus pursue her answer meet:—

My sire is of a noble line,
And my name is Geraldine:
Five warriors seized me yestermorn,
Me, even me, a maid forlorn:
They choked my cries with force and fright,
And tied me on a palfrey white.
The palfrey was as fleet as wind,
And they rode furiously behind.
They spurred amain, their steeds were white:
And once we crossed the shade of night.
As sure as Heaven shall rescue me,
I have no thought what men they be;
Nor do I know how long it is
(For I have lain entranced I wis)
Since one, the tallest of the five,
Took me from the palfrey's back,
A weary woman, scarce alive.

Some muttered words his comrades spoke:
Ha placed me underneath this oak;
He swore they would return with haste;
Whither they went I cannot tell—
I thought I heard, some minutes past,
Sounds as of a castle bell.
Stretch forth thy hand (thus ended she),
And help a wretched maid to flee.

Then Christabel stretched forth her hand,
And comforted fair Geraldine:
O well, bright dame! may you command
The service of Sir Leoline;
And gladly our stout chivalry
Will he send forth and friends withal
To guide and guard you safe and free
Home to your noble father's hall.

They crossed the moat, and Christabel
Took the key that fitted well;
A little door she opened straight,
All in the middle of the gate;
The gate that was ironed within and without,
Where an army in battle array had marched out.
The lady sank, belike through pain,
And Christabel with might and main
Lifted her up, a weary weight,
Over the threshold of the gate:
Then the lady rose again,
And moved, as she were not in pain.

They passed the hall, that echoes still,
Pass as lightly as you will!
The brands were flat, the brands were dying,
Amid their own white ashes lying;
But when the lady passed, there came
A tongue of light, a fit of flame;
And Christabel saw the lady's eye,
And nothing else saw she thereby,
Save the boss of the shield of Sir Leoline tall,

Which hung in a murky old niche in the wall.
O softly tread, said Christabel,
My father seldom sleepeth well.

 O weary lady, Geraldine,
I pray you, drink this cordial wine!
It is a wine of virtuous powers;
My mother made it of wild flowers.

And will your mother pity me,
Who am a maiden most forlorn?
Christabel answered—Woe is me!
She died the hour that I was born.
I have heard the grey-haired friar tell
How on her death-bed she did say,
That she should hear the castle-bell
Strike twelve upon my wedding-day.
O mother dear! that thou wert here!
I would, said Geraldine, she were!

But soon with altered voice, said she—
'Off, wandering mother! Peak and pine!
I have power to bid thee flee.'
Alas! what ails poor Geraldine?
Why stares she with unsettled eye?
Can she the bodiless dead espy?
And why with hollow voice cries she,
'Off, woman, off! this hour is mine—
Though thou her guardian spirit be,
Off, woman, off! 'tis given to me.'

And thus the lofty lady spake—
'All they who live in the upper sky,
Do love you, holy Christabel!
And you love them, and for their sake
And for the good which me befel,
Even I in my degree will try,
Fair maiden, to requite you well.
But now unrobe yourself; for I
Must pray, ere yet in bed I lie.'

Quoth Christabel, So let it be!
And as the lady bade, did she.
Her gentle limbs did she undress,
And lay down in her loveliness.

But through her brain of weal and woe
So many thoughts moved to and fro,
That vain it were her lids to close;
So half-way from the bed she rose,
And on her elbow did recline
To look at the lady Geraldine.

Beneath the lamp the lady bowed,
And slowly rolled her eyes around;
Then drawing in her breath aloud,
Like one that shuddered, she unbound
The cincture from beneath her breast:
Her silken robe, and inner vest,
Dropt to her feet, and full in view,
Behold! her bosom and half her side–
A sight to dream of, not to tell!
O shield her! shield sweet Christabel!

Yet Geraldine nor speaks nor stirs;
Ah! what a stricken look was hers!
Deep from within she seems half-way
To lift some weight with sick assay,
And eyes the maid and seeks delay;
Then suddenly, as one defied,
Collects herself in scorn and pride,
And lay down by the Maiden's side!–
And in her arms the maid she took,
        Ah wel-a-day!
And with low voice and doleful look
These words did say:
'In the touch of this bosom there worketh a spell,
Which is lord of thy utterance, Christabel!
Thou knowest to-night, and wilt know to-morrow,
This mark of my shame, this seal of my sorrow;
    But vainly thou warrest,

> For this is alone in
> Thy power to declare,
> That in the dim forest
> Thou heard'st a low moaning,
> And found'st a bright lady, surpassingly fair;
> And didst bring her home with thee in love and in charity,
> To shield her and shelter her from the damp air.'
>
> And see! the lady Christabel
> Gathers herself from out her trance;
> Her limbs relax, her countenance
> Grows sad and soft; the smooth thin lids
> Close o'er her eyes; and tears she sheds—
> Large tears that leave the lashes bright!
> And oft the while she seems to smile
> As infants at a sudden light!
>
> Yea, she doth smile, and she doth weep,
> Like a youthful hermitess,
> Beauteous in a wilderness,
> Who, praying always, prays in sleep.
> And, if she move unquietly,
> Perchance, 'tis but the blood so free
> Comes back and tingles in her feet.
> No doubt, she hath a vision sweet.
> What if her guardian spirit 'twere,
> What if she knew her mother near?
> But this she knows, in joys and woes,
> That saints will aid if men will call:
> For the blue sky bends over all!

GLOSSARY

crew – archaic past tense of 'crow'.

mastiff – one of the most ancient breeds of dog.

my lady – Sir Leoline's wife, who died soon after Christabel was born.

furlong – an old measurement of distance: 201.168 metres.

wan – pale and ill-looking.

sore – here, 'extreme'.

palfrey – a docile horse used for ordinary riding, especially by women.

fleet – quick.

amain – (archaic) at full speed.

I wis – (arcahic) I know.

cordial – a sweet fruit-flavoured drink.

peak and pine – to look ill and yearn intensely.

wildered – bewildered.

ere – (archaic) before.

weal and woe – an archaic expression equivalent to 'for good or evil'.

cincture – a girdle or belt.

assay – here, 'blessed', from Anglo-Saxon 'gesælig'.

wel-a-day – an archaic exclamation.

doleful – sad.

warrest – to make war.

tairn and rill – mountain lake and stream.

QUESTIONS

Analyse the verse form of the first five lines of the poem and say how it differs from most of the conventional poetry of the time, and from Coleridge's other poetry.

Bring together all the elements of gothic horror in Part I and discuss their effect, a) in creating atmosphere, and b) in building up a description of Geraldine.

What words and phrases build up a picture of the beauty and innocence of Christabel?

How does Coleridge build up suspense in the description of Geraldine entering the castle?

What words and phrases suggest that Geraldine has evil intentions regarding Christabel?

The poem is unfinished so we will never know what Geraldine

means by: "This mark of my shame, this seal of my sorrow". What do you think she means? What does it suggest about how the plot might develop?

How is the conflict between Geraldine and the spirit of Christabel's mother presented?

COMMENTARY

From the very first line of the poem we notice the unusual metre. Coleridge himself explains this in his introduction to the poem:

> I have only to add that the metre of Christabel is not, properly speaking, irregular, though it may seem so from its being founded on a new principle: namely, that of counting in each line the accents, not the syllables. Though the latter may vary from seven to twelve, yet in each line the accents will be found to be only four.

Actually, it is not a "new principle". The four stress line was the very basis of Old English poetry, and many traditional ballads are written with lines which have four stresses, but a varying number of syllables. Thus his choice of metre is appropriate to the medieval setting of his subject.

The tone of gothic horror is suggested in the first line by the clock striking midnight and the hooting of the owls. This is continued by the barking of the mastiff and the belief that she "sees my lady's shroud". Christabel is introduced in the next strophe, her piety emphasised by the fact that she is praying – however, it is not in church, but by a "huge, broad-breasted, old oak tree" covered with mistletoe (hints of the pagan religion that Christianity replaced). She is disturbed by a "damsel bright", whose description is disturbing: "the neck that made the white robe wan" – in other words, he skin is startlingly white. Her hair "wildly glittered" with gems, and it was "frightful" to see her. Geraldine explains her presence with an unlikely story of abduction by "five warriors", and pleads with Christabel to help her. When Christabel takes Geraldine to the castle there is further evidence of her supernatural nature: she is unable to pass through the gate: "The lady sank, belike through pain" and Christabel has to carry her across the threshold. "Then the lady rose again,/ And moved, as she were not in pain". This inability to cross thresholds is a feature of vampires in much horror literature. Also, when Geraldine goes into the hall, the "brands" (torches), which were dying out, flare up with "A tongue of light, a fit of flame" when Geraldine passed. Christabel gives Geraldine a drink of "cordial wine" which her mother made, and Geraldine seems to see her spirit, and tries to drive it away. The words "This hour is mine" are particularly chilling, as they suggest that Geraldine has some evil intention with regard to Christabel. Christabel's beauty is described as she undresses for bed, but there is something uncanny about Geraldine's body:

> Behold! her bosom and half her side–
> A sight to dream of, not to tell!
> O shield her! shield sweet Christabel!

Geraldine embraces Christabel in bed (some critics had detected lesbian connotations) and makes a disturbing prophecy:

> 'In the touch of this bosom there worketh a spell,
> Which is lord of thy utterance, Christabel!
> Thou knowest to-night, and wilt know to-morrow,
> This mark of my shame, this seal of my sorrow;

We find out in Part II, that Geraldine's spell does indeed control Christabel's power to speak, but, as the poem is unfinished, we never find out the details of Geraldine's "shame" and "sorrow". Christabel's innocence is emphasised by the words:

> And oft the while she seems to smile
> As infants at a sudden light!

Part I ends with a beautiful desciption of Christabel's dream of her "guardian spirit", her mother, watching over her.

SUMMARY OF PART II

The second part opens with the introduction of Geraldine to Sir Leoline, who recognizes in "the lofty lady" the daughter of his "friend in youth" Roland de Vaux of Tryermaine, who had become estranged many years ago after a quarrel. The baron is highly indignant when he hears Geraldine's story, and vows to avenge "the child of his friend". Meanwhile, poor Christabel is under a mysterious spell, cast on her by the "snake-like looks" of Geraldine. Sir Leoline, glad of the opportunity of a reconciliation to his long-lost friend, sends Bracy the bard to Roland's border castle, commissioning him to tell Lord Roland that his daughter is safe and to come to meet Sir Leoline and be friends once more. Bard Bracy hesitates on account of having dreamt that a dove (Christabel) had "a green snake...coiled around its wings and neck/...underneath the old tree" and having "vowed...with music strong and saintly song/ to exorcise the forest". When Christabel, pleads with him by her "mother's soul to send away that woman", he is confused, angry that his hospitality should be abused and, "in tones abrupt, austere" sends the reluctant Bracy on his mission.

PART II

The air is still! through mist and cloud
That merry peal comes ringing loud;
And Geraldine shakes off her dread,
And rises lightly from the bed;
Puts on her silken vestments white,
And tricks her hair in lovely plight,
And nothing doubting of her spell
Awakens the lady Christabel.
'Sleep you, sweet lady Christabel?
I trust that you have rested well.'

The lovely maid and the lady tall
Are pacing both into the hall,
And pacing on through page and groom,
Enter the Baron's presence-room.
The Baron rose, and while he prest
His gentle daughter to his breast,

With cheerful wonder in his eyes
The lady Geraldine espies,
And gave such welcome to the same,
As might beseem so bright a dame!

But when he heard the lady's tale,
And when she told her father's name,
Why waxed Sir Leoline so pale,
Murmuring o'er the name again,
Lord Roland de Vaux of Tryermaine?
Alas! they had been friends in youth;
But whispering tongues can poison truth;
And constancy lives in realms above;
And life is thorny; and youth is vain;
And to be wroth with one we love
Doth work like madness in the brain.
And thus it chanced, as I divine,
With Roland and Sir Leoline.
Each spake words of high disdain
And insult to his heart's best brother:
They parted—ne'er to meet again!
But never either found another
To free the hollow heart from paining—
They stood aloof, the scars remaining,
Like cliffs which had been rent asunder;
A dreary sea now flows between;—
But neither heat, nor frost, nor thunder,
Shall wholly do away, I ween,
The marks of that which once hath been.

Sir Leoline, a moment's space,
Stood gazing on the damsel's face:
And the youthful Lord of Tryermaine
Came back upon his heart again.

O then the Baron forgot his age,
His noble heart swelled high with rage;
He swore by the wounds in Jesu's side
He would proclaim it far and wide,
With trump and solemn heraldry,

That they, who thus had wronged the dame,
Were base as spotted infamy!
'And if they dare deny the same,
My herald shall appoint a week,
And let the recreant traitors seek
My tourney court—that there and then
I may dislodge their reptile souls
From the bodies and forms of men!'
He spake: his eye in lightning rolls!
For the lady was ruthlessly seized; and he kenned
In the beautiful lady the child of his friend!

And now the tears were on his face,
And fondly in his arms he took
Fair Geraldine, who met the embrace,
Prolonging it with joyous look.
Which when she viewed, a vision fell
Upon the soul of Christabel,
The vision of fear, the touch and pain!
She shrunk and shuddered, and saw again—
(Ah, woe is me! Was it for thee,
Thou gentle maid! such sights to see?)

Again she saw that bosom old,
Again she felt that bosom cold,
And drew in her breath with a hissing sound:
Whereat the Knight turned wildly round,
And nothing saw, but his own sweet maid
With eyes upraised, as one that prayed.

Nay, by my soul!' said Leoline.
'Ho! Bracy the bard, the charge be thine!
Go thou, with music sweet and loud,
And take two steeds with trappings proud,
And take the youth whom thou lov'st best
To bear thy harp, and learn thy song,
And clothe you both in solemn vest,
And over the mountains haste along,
Lest wandering folk, that are abroad,
Detain you on the valley road.

'And when he has crossed the Irthing flood,
My merry bard! he hastes, he hastes
Up Knorren Moor, through Halegarth Wood,
And reaches soon that castle good
Which stands and threatens Scotland's wastes.

'Bard Bracy! bard Bracy! your horses are fleet,
Ye must ride up the hall, your music so sweet,
More loud than your horses' echoing feet!
And loud and loud to Lord Roland call,
Thy daughter is safe in Langdale hall!
Thy beautiful daughter is safe and free–
Sir Leoline greets thee thus through me!
He bids thee come without delay
With all thy numerous array
And take thy lovely daughter home:
And he will meet thee on the way
With all his numerous array
White with their panting palfreys' foam:
And, by mine honour! I will say,
That I repent me of the day
When I spake words of fierce disdain
To Roland de Vaux of Tryermaine!–
–For since that evil hour hath flown,
Many a summer's sun hath shone;
Yet ne'er found I a friend again
Like Roland de Vaux of Tryermaine.'

The lady fell, and clasped his knees,
Her face upraised, her eyes o'erflowing;
And Bracy replied, with faltering voice,
His gracious Hail on all bestowing!–
'Thy words, thou sire of Christabel,
Are sweeter than my harp can tell;
Yet might I gain a boon of thee,
This day my journey should not be,
So strange a dream hath come to me,
That I had vowed with music loud
To clear yon wood from thing unblest,

Warned by a vision in my rest!
For in my sleep I saw that dove,
That gentle bird, whom thou dost love,
And call'st by thy own daughter's name—
Sir Leoline! I saw the same
Fluttering, and uttering fearful moan,
Among the green herbs in the forest alone.
Which when I saw and when I heard,
I wonder'd what might ail the bird;
For nothing near it could I see,
Save the grass and green herbs underneath the old tree.

'And in my dream methought I went
To search out what might there be found;
And what the sweet bird's trouble meant,
That thus lay fluttering on the ground.
I went and peered, and could descry
No cause for her distressful cry;
But yet for her dear lady's sake
I stooped, methought, the dove to take,
When lo! I saw a bright green snake
Coiled around its wings and neck.
Green as the herbs on which it couched,
Close by the dove's its head it crouched;
And with the dove it heaves and stirs,
Swelling its neck as she swelled hers!
I woke; it was the midnight hour,
The clock was echoing in the tower;
But though my slumber was gone by,
This dream it would not pass away—
It seems to live upon my eye!
And thence I vowed this self-same day
With music strong and saintly song
To wander through the forest bare,
Lest aught unholy loiter there.'

Thus Bracy said: the Baron, the while,
Half-listening heard him with a smile;
Then turned to Lady Geraldine,
His eyes made up of wonder and love;

And said in courtly accents fine,
'Sweet maid, Lord Roland's beauteous dove,
With arms more strong than harp or song,
Thy sire and I will crush the snake!'
He kissed her forehead as he spake,
And Geraldine in maiden wise
Casting down her large bright eyes,
With blushing cheek and courtesy fine
She turned her from Sir Leoline;
Softly gathering up her train,
That o'er her right arm fell again;
And folded her arms across her chest,
And couched her head upon her breast,
And looked askance at Christabel—
Jesu, Maria, shield her well!

Within the Baron's heart and brain
If thoughts, like these, had any share,
They only swelled his rage and pain,
And did but work confusion there.
His heart was cleft with pain and rage,
His cheeks they quivered, his eyes were wild,
Dishonoured thus in his old age;
Dishonoured by his only child,
And all his hospitality
To the wronged daughter of his friend
By more than woman's jealousy
Brought thus to a disgraceful end—
He rolled his eye with stern regard
Upon the gentle minstrel bard,
And said in tones abrupt, austere—
'Why, Bracy! dost thou loiter here?
I bade thee hence!' The bard obeyed;
And turning from his own sweet maid,
The agéd knight, Sir Leoline,
Led forth the lady Geraldine!

GLOSSARY

peal – the sound of bells.
waxed – grew (not a hair removal treatment for Sir Leoline's
    legs).
wroth – (archaic) angry.
divine – guess.
recreant – cowardly.
tourney – tournament.
kenned – (archaic) knew.
Irthing flood – River Irthing is a river in Cumbria
Knorren Moor/Halegarth Wood – these seem to be place
    names made up by Coleridge.
boon – gift or favour.
descry – to catch sight of.
askance – with look of suspicion or disapproval.

QUESTIONS

This part begins with regular tetrameters, but later on, some
irregular four-stressed lines are used. Find some examples and
consider their effect.

Coleridge uses many archaic words to build up the sense of a
medieval setting and a sense of gothic horror (though nowhere near
as many as in *The Ancient Mariner*). Make a list of these words and
discuss their effect (hint: several, though not all, may be found in
the glossary).

Explain the reason that Sir Leoline is "confused", and thus
unable to respond to the warning signs that might save his
daughter. Consider his feelings about his former friend, his
undoubted attraction to Geraldine, his response to Bracy's dream,
and his belief that he would be failing in the duty of hospitality if he
did not help her.

How is Geraldine developed as an evil creature in this poem?
What words and phrases suggest her evil, and her power? What is
her connection with the snake in Bracy's dream?

The poem is brought to life by many vivid adjectives and figures of speech. Find some examples and consider their effect.

COMMENTARY

Next day, Geraldine tells Sir Leoline that she is the daughter of Lord Roland de Vaux of Tryermaine, a former friend from whom Sir Leoline was estranged. The nature of the quarrel, its causes and its effects on Sir Leoline, are vividly described in the lines:

> ...to be wroth with one we love
> Doth work like madness in the brain.

This "madness", the chance of a reconciliation, and Geraldine's beauty, affect Sir Leonine's judgement, and he is determined to help Geraldine and be reconciled with his old friend. The strength of his determination is seen in these lines:

> His noble heart swelled high with rage;
> He swore by the wounds in Jesu's side

and the strong language he uses to describe "the recreant traitors":

> I may dislodge their reptile souls
> From the bodies and forms of men!'

There is a vivid description of Christabel's fear, heightened by frightening description of Geraldine:

> Again she saw that bosom old,
> Again she felt that bosom cold,
> And drew in her breath with a hissing sound...

Sir Leoline commands his bard, Bracy, to take a message to Lord Roland, and it is in vain that the bard tells him about a warning dream in which a snake coils round a dove, and the dove is Christabel. The dream is vividly described. The dove is "Fluttering, and uttering fearful moan,", as a "a bright green snake" coils around it. It is interesting that Geraldine hissed earlier in this passage, suggesting a connection with the snake. He asks permission to exorcise the evil in the forest with music but Sir Leoline refuses angrily. His confusion is vividly described:

> They only swelled his rage and pain,
> And did but work confusion there.
> His heart was cleft with pain and rage,
> His cheeks they quivered, his eyes were wild...

Thus Geraldine has her way.

There follows *The Conclusion to Part II*, which has nothing important to add, and there the poem ends – a tantalising fragment.

CHRISTABEL (FULL)

PART I

'Tis the middle of night by the castle clock,
And the owls have awakened the crowing cock;
Tu–whit!—Tu–whoo!
And hark, again! the crowing cock,
How drowsily it crew.   5
Sir Leoline, the Baron rich,
Hath a toothless mastiff bitch;
From her kennel beneath the rock
She maketh answer to the clock,
Four for the quarters, and twelve for the hour;   10
Ever and aye, by shine and shower,
Sixteen short howls, not over loud;
Some say, she sees my lady's shroud.

Is the night chilly and dark?
The night is chilly, but not dark.   15
The thin gray cloud is spread on high,
It covers but not hides the sky.
The moon is behind, and at the full;
And yet she looks both small and dull.
The night is chill, the cloud is gray: 20
'Tis a month before the month of May,
And the Spring comes slowly up this way.

The lovely lady, Christabel,
Whom her father loves so well,
What makes her in the wood so late,   25
A furlong from the castle gate?
She had dreams all yesternight
Of her own betrothéd knight;
And she in the midnight wood will pray
For the weal of her lover that's far away.   30

She stole along, she nothing spoke,
The sighs she heaved were soft and low,
And naught was green upon the oak
But moss and rarest misletoe:
She kneels beneath the huge oak tree,   35
And in silence prayeth she.

The lady sprang up suddenly,
The lovely lady, Christabel!
It moaned as near, as near can be,
But what it is she cannot tell.–   40
On the other side it seems to be,
Of the huge, broad-breasted, old oak tree.

The night is chill; the forest bare;
Is it the wind that moaneth bleak?
There is not wind enough in the air   45
To move away the ringlet curl
From the lovely lady's cheek–
There is not wind enough to twirl
The one red leaf, the last of its clan,
That dances as often as dance it can,   50
Hanging so light, and hanging so high,
On the topmost twig that looks up at the sky.

Hush, beating heart of Christabel!
Jesu, Maria, shield her well!
She folded her arms beneath her cloak,   55
And stole to the other side of the oak.
    What sees she there?

There she sees a damsel bright,
Drest in a silken robe of white,
That shadowy in the moonlight shone: 60
The neck that made that white robe wan,
Her stately neck, and arms were bare;
Her blue-veined feet unsandal'd were,
And wildly glittered here and there
The gems entangled in her hair.   65
I guess, 'twas frightful there to see
A lady so richly clad as she—
Beautiful exceedingly!

Mary mother, save me now!
(Said Christabel,) And who art thou?   70

The lady strange made answer meet,
And her voice was faint and sweet:–
Have pity on my sore distress,
I scarce can speak for weariness:
Stretch forth thy hand, and have no fear!   75
Said Christabel, How camest thou here?
And the lady, whose voice was faint and sweet,
Did thus pursue her answer meet:–

My sire is of a noble line,
And my name is Geraldine: 80
Five warriors seized me yestermorn,
Me, even me, a maid forlorn:
They choked my cries with force and fright,
And tied me on a palfrey white.
The palfrey was as fleet as wind,   85
And they rode furiously behind.
They spurred amain, their steeds were white:
And once we crossed the shade of night.
As sure as Heaven shall rescue me,
I have no thought what men they be;   90
Nor do I know how long it is
(For I have lain entranced I wis)
Since one, the tallest of the five,
Took me from the palfrey's back,

A weary woman, scarce alive.   95
Some muttered words his comrades spoke:
Ha placed me underneath this oak;
He swore they would return with haste;
Whither they went I cannot tell—
I thought I heard, some minutes past,   100
Sounds as of a castle bell.
Stretch forth thy hand (thus ended she),
And help a wretched maid to flee.

Then Christabel stretched forth her hand,
And comforted fair Geraldine: 105
O well, bright dame! may you command
The service of Sir Leoline;
And gladly our stout chivalry
Will he send forth and friends withal
To guide and guard you safe and free   110
Home to your noble father's hall.

She rose: and forth with steps they passed
That strove to be, and were not, fast.
Her gracious stars the lady blest,
And thus spake on sweet Christabel: 115
All our household are at rest,
The hall as silent as the cell;
Sir Leoline is weak in health,
And may not well awakened be,
But we will move as if in stealth,   120
And I beseech your courtesy,
This night, to share your couch with me.

They crossed the moat, and Christabel
Took the key that fitted well;
A little door she opened straight,   125
All in the middle of the gate;
The gate that was ironed within and without,
Where an army in battle array had marched out.
The lady sank, belike through pain,
And Christabel with might and main   130
Lifted her up, a weary weight,

Over the threshold of the gate:
Then the lady rose again,
And moved, as she were not in pain.

So free from danger, free from fear,   135
They crossed the court: right glad they were.
And Christabel devoutly cried
To the lady by her side,
Praise we the Virgin all divine
Who hath rescued thee from thy distress!   140
Alas, alas! said Geraldine,
I cannot speak for weariness.
So free from danger, free from fear,
They crossed the court: right glad they were.

Outside her kennel, the mastiff old   145
Lay fast asleep, in moonshine cold.
The mastiff old did not awake,
Yet she an angry moan did make!
And what can ail the mastiff bitch?
Never till now she uttered yell   150
Beneath the eye of Christabel.
Perhaps it is the owlet's scritch:
For what can ail the mastiff bitch?

They passed the hall, that echoes still,
Pass as lightly as you will!   155
The brands were flat, the brands were dying,
Amid their own white ashes lying;
But when the lady passed, there came
A tongue of light, a fit of flame;
And Christabel saw the lady's eye,   160
And nothing else saw she thereby,
Save the boss of the shield of Sir Leoline tall,
Which hung in a murky old niche in the wall.
O softly tread, said Christabel,
My father seldom sleepeth well.   165

Sweet Christabel her feet doth bare,
And jealous of the listening air

They steal their way from stair to stair,
Now in glimmer, and now in gloom,
And now they pass the Baron's room,   170
As still as death, with stifled breath!
And now have reached her chamber door;
And now doth Geraldine press down
The rushes of the chamber floor.

The moon shines dim in the open air,   175
And not a moonbeam enters here.
But they without its light can see
The chamber carved so curiously,
Carved with figures strange and sweet,
All made out of the carver's brain,   180
For a lady's chamber meet:
The lamp with twofold silver chain
Is fastened to an angel's feet.

The silver lamp burns dead and dim;
But Christabel the lamp will trim.   185
She trimmed the lamp, and made it bright,
And left it swinging to and fro,
While Geraldine, in wretched plight,
Sank down upon the floor below.

O weary lady, Geraldine,   190
I pray you, drink this cordial wine!
It is a wine of virtuous powers;
My mother made it of wild flowers.

And will your mother pity me,
Who am a maiden most forlorn?   195
Christabel answered—Woe is me!
She died the hour that I was born.
I have heard the grey-haired friar tell
How on her death-bed she did say,
That she should hear the castle-bell   200
Strike twelve upon my wedding-day.
O mother dear! that thou wert here!
I would, said Geraldine, she were!

But soon with altered voice, said she–
'Off, wandering mother! Peak and pine!   205
I have power to bid thee flee.'
Alas! what ails poor Geraldine?
Why stares she with unsettled eye?
Can she the bodiless dead espy?
And why with hollow voice cries she,   210
'Off, woman, off! this hour is mine–
Though thou her guardian spirit be,
Off, woman, off! 'tis given to me.'

Then Christabel knelt by the lady's side,
And raised to heaven her eyes so blue–   215
Alas! said she, this ghastly ride–
Dear lady! it hath wildered you!
The lady wiped her moist cold brow,
And faintly said, ''tis over now!'

Again the wild-flower wine she drank: 220
Her fair large eyes 'gan glitter bright,
And from the floor whereon she sank,
The lofty lady stood upright:
She was most beautiful to see,
Like a lady of a far countrée.   225

And thus the lofty lady spake–
'All they who live in the upper sky,
Do love you, holy Christabel!
And you love them, and for their sake
And for the good which me befel,   230
Even I in my degree will try,
Fair maiden, to requite you well.
But now unrobe yourself; for I
Must pray, ere yet in bed I lie.'

Quoth Christabel, So let it be!   235
And as the lady bade, did she.
Her gentle limbs did she undress,
And lay down in her loveliness.

But through her brain of weal and woe
So many thoughts moved to and fro,   240
That vain it were her lids to close;
So half-way from the bed she rose,
And on her elbow did recline
To look at the lady Geraldine.

Beneath the lamp the lady bowed,   245
And slowly rolled her eyes around;
Then drawing in her breath aloud,
Like one that shuddered, she unbound
The cincture from beneath her breast:
Her silken robe, and inner vest,   250
Dropt to her feet, and full in view,
Behold! her bosom and half her side—
A sight to dream of, not to tell!
O shield her! shield sweet Christabel!

Yet Geraldine nor speaks nor stirs;   255
Ah! what a stricken look was hers!
Deep from within she seems half-way
To lift some weight with sick assay,
And eyes the maid and seeks delay;
Then suddenly, as one defied,   260
Collects herself in scorn and pride,
And lay down by the Maiden's side!—
And in her arms the maid she took,
        Ah wel-a-day!
And with low voice and doleful look   265
These words did say:
'In the touch of this bosom there worketh a spell,
Which is lord of thy utterance, Christabel!
Thou knowest to-night, and wilt know to-morrow,
This mark of my shame, this seal of my sorrow;   270
    But vainly thou warrest,
      For this is alone in
    Thy power to declare,
      That in the dim forest
    Thou heard'st a low moaning,   275

And found'st a bright lady, surpassingly fair;
And didst bring her home with thee in love and in charity,
To shield her and shelter her from the damp air.'

THE CONCLUSION TO PART I

It was a lovely sight to see
The lady Christabel, when she   280
Was praying at the old oak tree.
   Amid the jaggéd shadows
   Of mossy leafless boughs,
   Kneeling in the moonlight,
   To make her gentle vows;   285
Her slender palms together prest,
Heaving sometimes on her breast;
Her face resigned to bliss or bale—
Her face, oh call it fair not pale,
And both blue eyes more bright than clear,   290
Each about to have a tear.

With open eyes (ah woe is me!)
Asleep, and dreaming fearfully,
Fearfully dreaming, yet, I wis,
Dreaming that alone, which is—   295
O sorrow and shame! Can this be she,
The lady, who knelt at the old oak tree?
And lo! the worker of these harms,
That holds the maiden in her arms,
Seems to slumber still and mild,   300
As a mother with her child.

A star hath set, a star hath risen,
O Geraldine! since arms of thine
Have been the lovely lady's prison.
O Geraldine! one hour was thine—   305
Thou'st had thy will! By tairn and rill,
The night-birds all that hour were still.
But now they are jubilant anew,
From cliff and tower, tu—whoo! tu—whoo!

Tu–whoo! tu–whoo! from wood and fell!   310

And see! the lady Christabel
Gathers herself from out her trance;
Her limbs relax, her countenance
Grows sad and soft; the smooth thin lids
Close o'er her eyes; and tears she sheds—   315
Large tears that leave the lashes bright!
And oft the while she seems to smile
As infants at a sudden light!

Yea, she doth smile, and she doth weep,
Like a youthful hermitess,   320
Beauteous in a wilderness,
Who, praying always, prays in sleep.
And, if she move unquietly,
Perchance, 'tis but the blood so free
Comes back and tingles in her feet.   325
No doubt, she hath a vision sweet.
What if her guardian spirit 'twere,
What if she knew her mother near?
But this she knows, in joys and woes,
That saints will aid if men will call: 330
For the blue sky bends over all!

(1797)

PART II

Each matin bell, the Baron saith,
Knells us back to a world of death.
These words Sir Leoline first said,
When he rose and found his lady dead: 335
These words Sir Leoline will say
Many a morn to his dying day!

And hence the custom and law began
That still at dawn the sacristan,
Who duly pulls the heavy bell,   340

Five and forty beads must tell
Between each stroke–a warning knell,
Which not a soul can choose but hear
From Bratha Head to Wyndermere.

Saith Bracy the bard, So let it knell!   345
And let the drowsy sacristan
Still count as slowly as he can!
There is no lack of such, I ween,
As well fill up the space between.
In Langdale Pike and Witch's Lair,   350
And Dungeon-ghyll so foully rent,
With ropes of rock and bells of air
Three sinful sextons' ghosts are pent,
Who all give back, one after t'other,
The death-note to their living brother;   355
And oft too, by the knell offended,
Just as their one! two! three! is ended,
The devil mocks the doleful tale
With a merry peal from Borodale.

The air is still! through mist and cloud   360
That merry peal comes ringing loud;
And Geraldine shakes off her dread,
And rises lightly from the bed;
Puts on her silken vestments white,
And tricks her hair in lovely plight,   365
And nothing doubting of her spell
Awakens the lady Christabel.
'Sleep you, sweet lady Christabel?
I trust that you have rested well.'

And Christabel awoke and spied   370
The same who lay down by her side–
O rather say, the same whom she
Raised up beneath the old oak tree!
Nay, fairer yet! and yet more fair!
For she belike hath drunken deep   375
Of all the blessedness of sleep!
And while she spake, her looks, her air

Such gentle thankfulness declare,
That (so it seemed) her girded vests
Grew tight beneath her heaving breasts. 380
'Sure I have sinn'd!' said Christabel,
'Now heaven be praised if all be well!'
And in low faltering tones, yet sweet,
Did she the lofty lady greet
With such perplexity of mind 385
As dreams too lively leave behind.

So quickly she rose, and quickly arrayed
Her maiden limbs, and having prayed
That He, who on the cross did groan,
Might wash away her sins unknown, 390
She forthwith led fair Geraldine
To meet her sire, Sir Leoline.

The lovely maid and the lady tall
Are pacing both into the hall,
And pacing on through page and groom, 395
Enter the Baron's presence-room.

The Baron rose, and while he prest
His gentle daughter to his breast,
With cheerful wonder in his eyes
The lady Geraldine espies, 400
And gave such welcome to the same,
As might beseem so bright a dame!

But when he heard the lady's tale,
And when she told her father's name,
Why waxed Sir Leoline so pale, 405
Murmuring o'er the name again,
Lord Roland de Vaux of Tryermaine?
Alas! they had been friends in youth;
But whispering tongues can poison truth;
And constancy lives in realms above; 410
And life is thorny; and youth is vain;
And to be wroth with one we love
Doth work like madness in the brain.

And thus it chanced, as I divine,
With Roland and Sir Leoline.   415
Each spake words of high disdain
And insult to his heart's best brother:
They parted–ne'er to meet again!
But never either found another
To free the hollow heart from paining–   420
They stood aloof, the scars remaining,
Like cliffs which had been rent asunder;
A dreary sea now flows between;–
But neither heat, nor frost, nor thunder,
Shall wholly do away, I ween,   425
The marks of that which once hath been.

Sir Leoline, a moment's space,
Stood gazing on the damsel's face:
And the youthful Lord of Tryermaine
Came back upon his heart again.   430

O then the Baron forgot his age,
His noble heart swelled high with rage;
He swore by the wounds in Jesu's side
He would proclaim it far and wide,
With trump and solemn heraldry,   435
That they, who thus had wronged the dame,
Were base as spotted infamy!
'And if they dare deny the same,
My herald shall appoint a week,
And let the recreant traitors seek   440
My tourney court–that there and then
I may dislodge their reptile souls
From the bodies and forms of men!'
He spake: his eye in lightning rolls!
For the lady was ruthlessly seized; and he kenned   445
In the beautiful lady the child of his friend!

And now the tears were on his face,
And fondly in his arms he took
Fair Geraldine, who met the embrace,
Prolonging it with joyous look.   450

Which when she viewed, a vision fell
Upon the soul of Christabel,
The vision of fear, the touch and pain!
She shrunk and shuddered, and saw again—
(Ah, woe is me! Was it for thee,   455
Thou gentle maid! such sights to see?)

Again she saw that bosom old,
Again she felt that bosom cold,
And drew in her breath with a hissing sound:
Whereat the Knight turned wildly round,   460
And nothing saw, but his own sweet maid
With eyes upraised, as one that prayed.

The touch, the sight, had passed away,
And in its stead that vision blest,
Which comforted her after-rest   465
While in the lady's arms she lay,
Had put a rapture in her breast,
And on her lips and o'er her eyes
Spread smiles like light!
     With new surprise,
'What ails then my belovéd child?'   470
The Baron said—His daughter mild
Made answer, 'All will yet be well!'
I ween, she had no power to tell
Aught else: so mighty was the spell.

Yet he, who saw this Geraldine,   475
Had deemed her sure a thing divine:
Such sorrow with such grace she blended,
As if she feared she had offended
Sweet Christabel, that gentle maid!
And with such lowly tones she prayed   480
She might be sent without delay
Home to her father's mansion.
     'Nay!
Nay, by my soul!' said Leoline.
'Ho! Bracy the bard, the charge be thine!
Go thou, with music sweet and loud,   485

And take two steeds with trappings proud,
And take the youth whom thou lov'st best
To bear thy harp, and learn thy song,
And clothe you both in solemn vest,
And over the mountains haste along,   490
Lest wandering folk, that are abroad,
Detain you on the valley road.

'And when he has crossed the Irthing flood,
My merry bard! he hastes, he hastes
Up Knorren Moor, through Halegarth Wood,   495
And reaches soon that castle good
Which stands and threatens Scotland's wastes.

'Bard Bracy! bard Bracy! your horses are fleet,
Ye must ride up the hall, your music so sweet,
More loud than your horses' echoing feet!   500
And loud and loud to Lord Roland call,
Thy daughter is safe in Langdale hall!
Thy beautiful daughter is safe and free—
Sir Leoline greets thee thus through me!
He bids thee come without delay   505
With all thy numerous array
And take thy lovely daughter home:
And he will meet thee on the way
With all his numerous array
White with their panting palfreys' foam: 510
And, by mine honour! I will say,
That I repent me of the day
When I spake words of fierce disdain
To Roland de Vaux of Tryermaine!—
—For since that evil hour hath flown,   515
Many a summer's sun hath shone;
Yet ne'er found I a friend again
Like Roland de Vaux of Tryermaine.'

The lady fell, and clasped his knees,
Her face upraised, her eyes o'erflowing;   520
And Bracy replied, with faltering voice,
His gracious Hail on all bestowing!—

'Thy words, thou sire of Christabel,
Are sweeter than my harp can tell;
Yet might I gain a boon of thee,   525
This day my journey should not be,
So strange a dream hath come to me,
That I had vowed with music loud
To clear yon wood from thing unblest,
Warned by a vision in my rest!   530
For in my sleep I saw that dove,
That gentle bird, whom thou dost love,
And call'st by thy own daughter's name—
Sir Leoline! I saw the same
Fluttering, and uttering fearful moan,   535
Among the green herbs in the forest alone.
Which when I saw and when I heard,
I wonder'd what might ail the bird;
For nothing near it could I see,
Save the grass and green herbs underneath the old tree.

'And in my dream methought I went   541
To search out what might there be found;
And what the sweet bird's trouble meant,
That thus lay fluttering on the ground.
I went and peered, and could descry   545
No cause for her distressful cry;
But yet for her dear lady's sake
I stooped, methought, the dove to take,
When lo! I saw a bright green snake
Coiled around its wings and neck.   550
Green as the herbs on which it couched,
Close by the dove's its head it crouched;
And with the dove it heaves and stirs,
Swelling its neck as she swelled hers!
I woke; it was the midnight hour,   555
The clock was echoing in the tower;
But though my slumber was gone by,
This dream it would not pass away—
It seems to live upon my eye!
And thence I vowed this self-same day   560
With music strong and saintly song

To wander through the forest bare,
Lest aught unholy loiter there.'

Thus Bracy said: the Baron, the while,
Half-listening heard him with a smile;   565
Then turned to Lady Geraldine,
His eyes made up of wonder and love;
And said in courtly accents fine,
'Sweet maid, Lord Roland's beauteous dove,
With arms more strong than harp or song,   570
Thy sire and I will crush the snake!'
He kissed her forehead as he spake,
And Geraldine in maiden wise
Casting down her large bright eyes,
With blushing cheek and courtesy fine   575
She turned her from Sir Leoline;
Softly gathering up her train,
That o'er her right arm fell again;
And folded her arms across her chest,
And couched her head upon her breast,   580
And looked askance at Christabel–
Jesu, Maria, shield her well!

A snake's small eye blinks dull and shy;
And the lady's eyes they shrunk in her head,
Each shrunk up to a serpent's eye,   585
And with somewhat of malice, and more of dread,
At Christabel she looked askance!–
One moment–and the sight was fled!
But Christabel in dizzy trance
Stumbling on the unsteady ground   590
Shuddered aloud, with a hissing sound;
And Geraldine again turned round,
And like a thing, that sought relief,
Full of wonder and full of grief,
She rolled her large bright eyes divine   595
Wildly on Sir Leoline.

The maid, alas! her thoughts are gone,
She nothing sees–no sight but one!

The maid, devoid of guile and sin,
I know not how, in fearful wise,   600
So deeply had she drunken in
That look, those shrunken serpent eyes,
That all her features were resigned
To this sole image in her mind:
And passively did imitate   605
That look of dull and treacherous hate!
And thus she stood, in dizzy trance,
Still picturing that look askance
With forced unconscious sympathy
Full before her father's view—   610
As far as such a look could be
In eyes so innocent and blue!

And when the trance was o'er, the maid
Paused awhile, and inly prayed:
Then falling at the Baron's feet,   615
'By my mother's soul do I entreat
That thou this woman send away!'
She said: and more she could not say:
For what she knew she could not tell,
O'er-mastered by the mighty spell.   620

Why is thy cheek so wan and wild,
Sir Leoline? Thy only child
Lies at thy feet, thy joy, thy pride,
So fair, so innocent, so mild;
The same, for whom thy lady died!   625
O by the pangs of her dear mother
Think thou no evil of thy child!
For her, and thee, and for no other,
She prayed the moment ere she died:
Prayed that the babe for whom she died,   630
Might prove her dear lord's joy and pride!
  That prayer her deadly pangs beguiled,
    Sir Leoline!
  And wouldst thou wrong thy only child,
    Her child and thine?   635

Within the Baron's heart and brain
If thoughts, like these, had any share,
They only swelled his rage and pain,
And did but work confusion there.
His heart was cleft with pain and rage,   640
His cheeks they quivered, his eyes were wild,
Dishonoured thus in his old age;
Dishonoured by his only child,
And all his hospitality
To the wronged daughter of his friend   645
By more than woman's jealousy
Brought thus to a disgraceful end—
He rolled his eye with stern regard
Upon the gentle minstrel bard,
And said in tones abrupt, austere—   650
'Why, Bracy! dost thou loiter here?
I bade thee hence!' The bard obeyed;
And turning from his own sweet maid,
The agéd knight, Sir Leoline,
Led forth the lady Geraldine!   655

(1800)

THE CONCLUSION TO PART II

A little child, a limber elf,
Singing, dancing to itself,
A fairy thing with red round cheeks,
That always finds, and never seeks,
Makes such a vision to the sight   660
As fills a father's eyes with light;
And pleasures flow in so thick and fast
Upon his heart, that he at last
Must needs express his love's excess
With words of unmeant bitterness.   665
Perhaps 'tis pretty to force together
Thoughts so all unlike each other;
To mutter and mock a broken charm,
To dally with wrong that does no harm.

Perhaps 'tis tender too and pretty   670
At each wild word to feel within
A sweet recoil of love and pity.
And what, if in a world of sin
(O sorrow and shame should this be true!)
Such giddiness of heart and brain   675
Comes seldom save from rage and pain,
So talks as it's most used to do.

(1801)

QUESTIONS

Analyse the verse form of one of the sections not included in the 'lite' version.

How do the additional descriptions in the full version of the poem help to build up the atmosphere of gothic horror?

Collect additional examples of archaic vocabulary and say how they contribute to the tone and atmosphere of the poem.

In the full version we get a much clear picture of Christabel. Write a description of her appearance and character.

Do the same for Geraldine.

How does Coleridge present the theme of good versus evil? Which has the upper hand at the end of Part II? Which do you think will triumph in the end?

Coleridge uses many symbols to suggest the supernatural, good an evil. List all the symbols you can find under those three headings, then comment on their effect.

How do you think Sir Leoline's regret over his broken friendship with Lord Roland contributed to the decisions he made?

How does Coleridge's use of repetition add dramatic power to the tale?

Coleridge's published *Christabel* with a Preface (see page 112). What key points does he make, and why does he think a preface was necessary?

"Every word tells; every line is a picture." (Tupper, 1838). Find and comment on examples which justify this statement.

Read an extract from Tupper's continuation of *Christabel* on page 113, and compare and contrast it with the original? How successful has Tupper been in imitating Coleridge's style?

Read *Carmilla* by Joseph Sheridan Le Fanu, and compare and contrast the characters and plot.

COMMENTARY

This is arguably Coleridge's finest poem – or would have been if he had managed to complete it. This is what Tupper (who wrote a continuation of the poem in 1838) had to say about it:

> Every word tells; every line is a picture: simple, beautiful, and imaginative, it retains its hold upon the mind by so many delicate feelers and touching points, that to outline harshly the main branches of the tree, would seem to be doing the injustice of neglect to the elegance of its foliage, and the microscopic perfection of every single leaf.

However, Coleridge was unable to finish the poem, though he worked on the poem on two separate occasions (see Preface on page 112). He was not helped by the fact that Wordsworth said the poem was unsuitable for inclusion in *Lyrical Ballads* (though even in its unfinished state it is far superior to some of Wordsworth's banalities (for example, *Michael*). It is easy to blame Coleridge's opium addiction, though, as with Kubla Khan, the influence of opium may have contributed to its other-wordly effect. It is probably more to do with Coleridge self-doubt (which was probably exacerbated by opium and Wordsworth's disapproval).

It was left to Martin Farquhar Tupper (1810–1889) to finish the poem, which he did in 1838 in a poem entitled *Geraldine*. Though he is a minor poet, he has nevertheless managed to capture the style of Coleridge's verse. An extract is given in the *Extras* below. The story has inspired others, in particular that Joseph Sheridan Le Fanu, whose novel *Carmilla* (1872) is an adaptation of *Christabel*. You might also enjoy watching the film *Twins of Evil* (1971) which was, in turn, inspired by *Carmilla* (warning – contains nudity, so don't show in class!)

CHRISTABEL EXTRAS

PREFACE

The first part of the following poem was written in the year 1797, at Stowey, in the county of Somerset. The second part, after my return from Germany, in the year 1800, at Keswick, Cumberland. It is probable that if the poem had been finished at either of the former periods, or if even the first and second part had been published in the year 1800, the impression of its originality would have been much greater than I dare at present expect. But for this I have only my own indolence to blame. The dates are mentioned for the exclusive purpose of precluding charges of plagiarism or servile imitation from myself. For there is amongst us a set of critics, who seem to hold, that every possible thought and image is traditional; who have no notion that there are such things as fountains in the world, small as well as great; and who would therefore charitably derive every rill they behold flowing, from a perforation made in some other man's tank. I am confident, however, that as far as the present poem is concerned, the celebrated poets whose writings I might be suspected of having imitated, either in particular passages, or in the tone and the spirit of the whole, would be among the first to vindicate me from the charge, and who, on any striking coincidence, would permit me to address them in this doggerel version of two monkish Latin hexameters.

'Tis mine and it is likewise yours;
But an if this will not do;

Let it be mine, good friend! for I
Am the poorer of the two.

I have only to add that the metre of Christabel is not, properly speaking, irregular, though it may seem so from its being founded on a new principle: namely, that of counting in each line the accents, not the syllables. Though the latter may vary from seven to twelve, yet in each line the accents will be found to be only four. Nevertheless, this occasional variation in number of syllables is not introduced wantonly, or for the mere ends of convenience, but in correspondence with some transition in the nature of the imagery or passion.

GERALDINE

A SEQUEL TO COLERIDGE'S CHRISTABEL
by Martin Farquhar Tupper, 1838

PART I.

(BEING THE THIRD OF CHRISTABEL.)

It is the wolf, on stealthy prowl,
Hath startled the night with a dismal howl,
It is the raven, whose hoarse croak
Comes like a groan from the sear old oak,
It is the owl, whose curdling screech
Hath peopled with terrors the spectral beech ;
For again the clock hath toll'd out twelve.
And sent to their gambols the gnome and the eh
And awoken the friar his beads to tell.
And taught the magician the time for his spell,
And to her cauldon hath hurried the witch.
And arous'd the deep bay of the mastiff bitch

The gibbous moon, all chilling and wan.
Like a sleepless eyeball looketh on,
Like an eyeball of sorrow behind a shroud
Forth looketh she from a torn grey cloud.

Pouring sad radiance on the black air, —
Sun of the night, — what sees she there r
O lonely one, O lovely one,
What dost thou here in the forest dun
Fair truant, — like an angel of light
Hiding from heaven in deep midnight r
Alas ! there is guilt in thy glittering eye
As fearfully dark it looks up to the sky-
Alas ! a dull unearthly light
Like a dead star, bluely white,
A seal of sin, I note it now,
Flickers upon thy ghastly brow ;
And about the huge old oak
Thickly curls a poisonous smoke.
And terrible shapes with evil names
Are leaping around a circle of flames,
And the tost air whirls, storm-driven,
And the rent earth quakes, charm-riven, —
And — art thou not afraid ?

The full version can be read online here:

https://archive.org/details/ger00aldinesequelttupprich/page/n3

THE NIGHTINGALE

A CONVERSATION POEM, APRIL, 1798

No cloud, no relique of the sunken day
Distinguishes the West, no long thin slip
Of sullen light, no obscure trembling hues.
Come, we will rest on this old mossy bridge!
You see the glimmer of the stream beneath,   5
But hear no murmuring: it flows silently,
O'er its soft bed of verdure. All is still,
A balmy night! and though the stars be dim,
Yet let us think upon the vernal showers
That gladden the green earth, and we shall find   10
A pleasure in the dimness of the stars.
And hark! the Nightingale begins its song,
'Most musical, most melancholy' bird!
A melancholy bird? Oh! idle thought!
In Nature there is nothing melancholy.   15
But some night-wandering man whose heart was pierced
With the remembrance of a grievous wrong,
Or slow distemper, or neglected love,
(And so, poor wretch! filled all things with himself,
And made all gentle sounds tell back the tale   20
Of his own sorrow) he, and such as he,
First named these notes a melancholy strain.
And many a poet echoes the conceit;

Poet who hath been building up the rhyme
When he had better far have stretched his limbs 25
Beside a brook in mossy forest-dell,
By sun or moon-light, to the influxes
Of shapes and sounds and shifting elements
Surrendering his whole spirit, of his song
And of his fame forgetful! so his fame 30
Should share in Nature's immortality,
A venerable thing! and so his song
Should make all Nature lovelier, and itself
Be loved like Nature! But 'twill not be so;
And youths and maidens most poetical, 35
Who lose the deepening twilights of the spring
In ball-rooms and hot theatres, they still
Full of meek sympathy must heave their sighs
O'er Philomela's pity-pleading strains.

My Friend, and thou, our Sister! we have learnt 40
A different lore: we may not thus profane
Nature's sweet voices, always full of love
And joyance! 'Tis the merry Nightingale
That crowds, and hurries, and precipitates
With fast thick warble his delicious notes, 45
As he were fearful that an April night
Would be too short for him to utter forth
His love-chant, and disburthen his full soul
Of all its music!

       And I know a grove
Of large extent, hard by a castle huge, 50
Which the great lord inhabits not; and so
This grove is wild with tangling underwood,
And the trim walks are broken up, and grass,
Thin grass and king-cups grow within the paths.
But never elsewhere in one place I knew 55
So many nightingales; and far and near,
In wood and thicket, over the wide grove,
They answer and provoke each other's song,
With skirmish and capricious passagings,
And murmurs musical and swift jug jug, 60

And one low piping sound more sweet than all—
Stirring the air with such a harmony,
That should you close your eyes, you might almost
Forget it was not day! On moonlight bushes,
Whose dewy leaflets are but half-disclosed.   65
You may perchance behold them on the twigs,
Their bright, bright eyes, their eyes both bright and full,
Glistening, while many a glow-worm in the shade
Lights up her love-torch.

        A most gentle Maid,
Who dwelleth in her hospitable home   70
Hard by the castle, and at latest eve
(Even like a Lady vowed and dedicate
To something more than Nature in the grove)
Glides through the pathways; she knows all their notes,
That gentle Maid! and oft, a moment's space,   75
What time the moon was lost behind a cloud,
Hath heard a pause of silence; till the moon
Emerging, hath awakened earth and sky
With one sensation, and those wakeful birds
Have all burst forth in choral minstrelsy,   80
As if some sudden gale had swept at once
A hundred airy harps! And she hath watched
Many a nightingale perch giddily
On blossomy twig still swinging from the breeze,
And to that motion tune his wanton song   85
Like tipsy Joy that reels with tossing head.

Farewell, O Warbler! till to-morrow eve,
And you, my friends! farewell, a short farewell!
We have been loitering long and pleasantly,
And now for our dear homes.—That strain again!   90
Full fain it would delay me! My dear babe,
Who, capable of no articulate sound,
Mars all things with his imitative lisp,
How he would place his hand beside his ear,
His little hand, the small forefinger up,   95
And bid us listen! And I deem it wise
To make him Nature's play-mate. He knows well

The evening-star; and once, when he awoke
In most distressful mood (some inward pain
Had made up that strange thing, an infant's dream–)   100
I hurried with him to our orchard-plot,
And he beheld the moon, and, hushed at once,
Suspends his sobs, and laughs most silently,
While his fair eyes, that swam with undropped tears,
Did glitter in the yellow moon-beam! Well!–   105
It is a father's tale: But if that Heaven
Should give me life, his childhood shall grow up
Familiar with these songs, that with the night
He may associate joy.–Once more, farewell,
Sweet Nightingale! once more, my friends! farewell.   110

(1798)

GLOSSARY

relique – here, 'remnant'.

verdure – lush green vegetation.

vernal – to do with Spring.

distemper – here, 'a bad mood'.

Philomela – an Athenian princess in Greek mythology raped and deprived of her tongue by her brother-in-law Tereus, avenged by the killing of his son, and changed into a nightingale while fleeing from him.

lore – traditional knowledge or belief.

profane – treat with disrespect.

precipitate – cause something to happen suddenly.

disburthen – unburden.

king-cups – a small to medium size perennial herbaceous plant of the buttercup family.

jug jug – According to legend, the "jug jug jug" of the nightingale's call echoes the bloody stump of Philomela's tongue as she tries without success to ward off Tereus.

perchance – perhaps.

dear babe – his first son, Hartley Coleridge (1796-1849).

QUESTIONS

The poem is written in blank verse (unrhymed iambic pentameter). Select any four lines and underline the stressed an unstressed syllables.

Compare the style and language of this poem with the poem by Gray on pages 6-7. Comment on the difference.

How does Coleridge evoke the beauty of nature in lines 1-33?

Why do "youths and maidens" miss out on the beauties of nature? How does this cause them to misinterpret the Nightingale? (see the note on Philomela and research the Greek myth).

What is the "different lore" that Coleridge and his sister have learned? How is it expressed in the poem?

What gothic elements can you find in the strophe from lines 69-86? What is your reaction to the "Maid"? Do you empathise with her moonlit walks, or see her as slightly mad?

Taking the poem as a whole, write about all the language that expresses the beauty of the nightingale and his song.

What views about the beneficent effect of Nature on mankind are expressed in this poem? If Coleridge had seen "Nature red in tooth and claw" on the African Savannah, would his philosophy have been the same?

How does the anecdote about his son, Hartley, help to express his message in this poem?

How far do you agree with those critics who find the poem rather bland? In what sense is this very blandness revolutionary at this period?

COMMENTARY

The Nightingale is one of the poem that Coleridge contributed to *Lyrical Ballads*. As it is one of his "conversation poems", it is written in conversational style, and at first reading, may seem rather bland, especially when compared to Milton's melancholy *Il Penseroso*:

> Sweet bird that shunn'st the noise of folly,
> Most musical, most melancholy!
> Thee, chauntress, oft the woods among,
> I woo to hear thy even-song;
> And missing thee, I walk unseen
> On the dry smooth-shaven green,
> To behold the wand'ring Moon,

or Keat's intense *Ode to a Nightingale*:

> Away! away! for I will fly to thee,
>   Not charioted by Bacchus and his pards,
> But on the viewless wings of Poesy,
>   Though the dull brain perplexes and retards.

The poet, Southey, described *The Nightingale* as "tolerable" - which is faint praise indeed.

However, we need to see the poem in context. Wordsworth and Coleridge were reacting against the over-ornate poetry of the 18th century (like the example on pages 6-7), and the deliberately low key, almost throwaway, conversational style sets a new benchmark for poetry in the way that the free verse of Ezra Pound and T S Eliot did in the early 20th century.

The poem begins with a description of a night that has just fallen. It is a beautiful description created by referring to telling details such as the "old mossy bridge", the "glimmer of the stream", the "soft bed of verdure". There is a touch of personification in the idea that the showers "gladden the green earth". He goes on to describe the song of the nightingale. He quotes a line from Milton's *Il Penseroso* "Most musical, most melancholy!" and then goes on to refute it with the words: "In

Nature there is nothing melancholy". He goes on to explain that any melancholy felt by humans is inside them:

> And so, poor wretch! filled all things with himself,
> And made all gentle sounds tell back the tale
> Of his own sorrow...

He goes on to say that such a person would do better to appreciate the beauty of nature, which is exemplified by more description: "forest-dell,/ By sun or moon-light". Instead, most "youths and maidens" prefer "ball-rooms and hot theatres" and only have an artificial, literary experience of the Nightingale as the Philomela of Greek myth.

In the next strophe he addresses his sister, saying that they have learned "a different lore". There follows a beautiful description of the nightingale, made up primarily of an enumeration of adjectives, with the emphasis on the joyousness of his music, in such words as "joyance" (referring to all Nature's voices) "merry" and "love chant".

The next strophe describes a huge neglected castle, the grounds of which have run wild. There are some mildly gothic elements in the description; "the grove is wild", "tangling underwood", "trim walks are broken up", but the main point is that it is full of nightingales. They are described as creatures of great beauty. The "jug jug" sound, associated with the Philomela myth of rape, is here given quite different connotations. It is "musical" and "sweet". The word "bright" is repeated three times in the description of the nightingales, and their light is linked to the "love-torch" of the glow worms. In the next strophe a highly evocative simile is used to describe their song: "As if some sudden gale had swept at once/ A hundred airy harps!". The strophe ends with an expression of the joy of the nightingales: "tipsy Joy that reels with tossing head", the word "tipsy" suggesting that the nightingale is drunk with the joy of singing his song – all this direct evidence from nature is used to contradict the literary association of the nightingale with melancholy.

The "Maid" in this strophe is also worth a mention. She is an unknown woman who is of the same mind as Coleridge (she would rather wander around at night listening to nightingales than go to ballrooms or theatres), though, once again, there is a touch of the gothic: an eccentric woman from a neglected castle wandering around at night.

In the final strophe, Coleridge bids farewell to the "Warbler" and promises to be there again on the following evening. He goes on to mention his "babe", Hartley, and relates an incident where the sight of the moon "hushed... his sobs", which he sees as evidence of the beneficent effect of Nature. He ends by saying that he hopes his son will be "familiar" with the nightingale's song as he grows up, and associate it with joy.

FEARS IN SOLITUDE

WRITTEN IN APRIL 1798, DURING THE
ALARM OF AN INVASION

A green and silent spot, amid the hills,
A small and silent dell! O'er stiller place
No singing sky-lark ever poised himself.
The hills are heathy, save that swelling slope,
Which hath a gay and gorgeous covering on,   5
All golden with the never-bloomless furze,
Which now blooms most profusely: but the dell,
Bathed by the mist, is fresh and delicate
As vernal corn-field, or the unripe flax,
When, through its half-transparent stalks, at eve,   10
The level sunshine glimmers with green light.
Oh! 'tis a quiet spirit-healing nook!
Which all, methinks, would love; but chiefly he,
The humble man, who, in his youthful years,
Knew just so much of folly, as had made   15
His early manhood more securely wise!
Here he might lie on fern or withered heath,
While from the singing lark (that sings unseen
The minstrelsy that solitude loves best),
And from the sun, and from the breezy air,   20
Sweet influences trembled o'er his frame;
And he, with many feelings, many thoughts,

Made up a meditative joy, and found
Religious meanings in the forms of Nature!
And so, his senses gradually wrapt   25
In a half sleep, he dreams of better worlds,
And dreaming hears thee still, O singing lark,
That singest like an angel in the clouds!

  My God! it is a melancholy thing
For such a man, who would full fain preserve   30
His soul in calmness, yet perforce must feel
For all his human brethren–O my God!
It weighs upon the heart, that he must think
What uproar and what strife may now be stirring
This way or that way o'er these silent hills–   35
Invasion, and the thunder and the shout,
And all the crash of onset; fear and rage,
And undetermined conflict–even now,
Even now, perchance, and in his native isle:
Carnage and groans beneath this blessed sun!   40
We have offended, Oh! my countrymen!
We have offended very grievously,
And been most tyrannous. From east to west
A groan of accusation pierces Heaven!
The wretched plead against us; multitudes   45
Countless and vehement, the sons of God,
Our brethren! Like a cloud that travels on.
Steamed up from Cairo's swamps of pestilence,
Even so, my countrymen! have we gone forth
And borne to distant tribes slavery and pangs,   50
And, deadlier far, our vices, whose deep taint
With slow perdition murders the whole man,
His body and his soul! Meanwhile, at home,
All individual dignity and power
Engulfed in Courts, Committees, Institutions,   55
Associations and Societies,
A vain, speech-mouthing, speech-reporting Guild,
One Benefit-Club for mutual flattery,
We have drunk up, demure as at a grace,
Pollutions from the brimming cup of wealth;   60
Contemptuous of all honourable rule,

Yet bartering freedom and the poor man's life
For gold, as at a market! The sweet words
Of Christian promise, words that even yet
Might stem destruction, were they wisely preached,   65
Are muttered o'er by men, whose tones proclaim
How flat and wearisome they feel their trade:
Rank scoffers some, but most too indolent
To deem them falsehoods or to know their truth.
Oh! blasphemous! the Book of Life is made   70
A superstitious instrument, on which
We gabble o'er the oaths we mean to break;
For all must swear—all and in every place,
College and wharf, council and justice-court;
All, all must swear, the briber and the bribed,   75
Merchant and lawyer, senator and priest,
The rich, the poor, the old man and the young;
All, all make up one scheme of perjury,
That faith doth reel; the very name of God
Sounds like a juggler's charm; and, bold with joy,   80
Forth from his dark and lonely hiding-place,
(Portentous sight!) the owlet Atheism,
Sailing on obscene wings athwart the noon,
Drops his blue-fringéd lids, and holds them close,
And hooting at the glorious sun in Heaven,   85
Cries out, 'Where is it?'

          Thankless too for peace,
(Peace long preserved by fleets and perilous seas)
Secure from actual warfare, we have loved
To swell the war-whoop, passionate for war!
Alas! for ages ignorant of all   90
Its ghastlier workings, (famine or blue plague,
Battle, or siege, or flight through wintry snows,)
We, this whole people, have been clamorous
For war and bloodshed; animating sports,
The which we pay for as a thing to talk of,   95
Spectators and not combatants! No guess
Anticipative of a wrong unfelt,
No speculation on contingency,
However dim and vague, too vague and dim

To yield a justifying cause; and forth,   100
(Stuffed out with big preamble, holy names.
And adjurations of the God in Heaven.)
We send our mandates for the certain death
Of thousands and ten thousands! Boys and girls,
And women, that would groan to see a child   105
Pull off an insect's leg, all read of war,
The best amusement for our morning meal!
The poor wretch, who has learnt his only prayers
From curses, who knows scarcely words enough
To ask a blessing from his Heavenly Father,   110
Becomes a fluent phraseman, absolute
And technical in victories and defeats,
And all our dainty terms for fratricide;
Terms which we trundle smoothly o'er our tongues
Like mere abstractions, empty sounds to which   115
We join no feeling and attach no form!
As if the soldier died without a wound;
As if the fibres of this godlike frame
Were gored without a pang; as if the wretch,
Who fell in battle, doing bloody deeds,   120
Passed off to Heaven, translated and not killed;
As though he had no wife to pine for him,
No God to judge him! Therefore, evil days
Are coming on us, O my countrymen!
And what if all-avenging Providence,   125
Strong and retributive, should make us know
The meaning of our words, force us to feel
The desolation and the agony
Of our fierce doings?

            Spare us yet awhile,
Father and God! O! spare us yet awhile!   130
Oh! let not English women drag their flight
Fainting beneath the burthen of their babes,
Of the sweet infants, that but yesterday
Laughed at the breast! Sons, brothers, husbands, all
Who ever gazed with fondness on the forms   135
Which grew up with you round the same fire-side,
And all who ever heard the sabbath-bells

Without the infidel's scorn, make yourselves pure!
Stand forth! be men! repel an impious foe,
Impious and false, a light yet cruel race,   140
Who laugh away all virtue, mingling mirth
With deeds of murder; and still promising
Freedom, themselves too sensual to be free,
Poison life's amities, and cheat the heart
Of faith and quiet hope, and all that soothes,   145
And all that lifts the spirit! Stand we forth;
Render them back upon the insulted ocean,
And let them toss as idly on its waves
As the vile sea-weed, which some mountain-blast
Swept from our shores! And oh! may we return   150
Not with a drunken triumph, but with fear,
Repenting of the wrongs with which we stung
So fierce a foe to frenzy!

          I have told,
O Britons! O my brethren! I have told
Most bitter truth, but without bitterness.   155
Nor deem my zeal or factious or mistimed;
For never can true courage dwell with them,
Who, playing tricks with conscience, dare not look
At their own vices. We have been too long
Dupes of a deep delusion! Some, belike,   160
Groaning with restless enmity, expect
All change from change of constituted power;
As if a Government had been a robe,
On which our vice and wretchedness were tagged
Like fancy-points and fringes, with the robe   165
Pulled off at pleasure. Fondly these attach
A radical causation to a few
Poor drudges of chastising Providence,
Who borrow all their hues and qualities
From our own folly and rank wickedness,   170
Which gave them birth and nursed them. Others, meanwhile,
Dote with a mad idolatry; and all
Who will not fall before their images,
And yield them worship, they are enemies
Even of their country!

175

Such have I been deemed.–
But, O dear Britain! O my Mother Isle!
Needs must thou prove a name most dear and holy
To me, a son, a brother, and a friend,
A husband, and a father! who revere
All bonds of natural love, and find them all
Within the limits of thy rocky shores.
O native Britain! O my Mother Isle!
How shouldst thou prove aught else but dear and holy
To me, who from thy lakes and mountain-hills,
Thy clouds, thy quiet dales, thy rocks and seas,
Have drunk in all my intellectual life,
All sweet sensations, all ennobling thoughts,
All adoration of the God in nature,
All lovely and all honourable things.
Whatever makes this mortal spirit feel
The joy and greatness of its future being?
There lives nor form nor feeling in my soul
Unborrowed from my country! O divine
And beauteous island! thou hast been my sole
And most magnificent temple, in the which
I walk with awe, and sing my stately songs,
Loving the God that made me!–

May my fears,
My filial fears, be vain! and may the vaunts
And menace of the vengeful enemy
Pass like the gust, that roared and died away
In the distant tree: which heard, and only heard
In this low dell, bowed not the delicate grass.

But now the gentle dew-fall sends abroad
The fruit-like perfume of the golden furze:
The light has left the summit of the hill,
Though still a sunny gleam lies beautiful,
Aslant the ivied beacon. Now farewell,
Farewell, awhile, O soft and silent spot!
On the green sheep-track, up the heathy hill,
Homeward I wind my way; and lo! recalled

From bodings that have well-nigh wearied me,
I find myself upon the brow, and pause
Startled! And after lonely sojourning
In such a quiet and surrounded nook,
This burst of prospect, here the shadowy main,   215
Dim-tinted, there the mighty majesty
Of that huge amphitheatre of rich
And elmy fields, seems like society–
Conversing with the mind, and giving it
A livelier impulse and a dance of thought!   220
And now, beloved Stowey! I behold
Thy church-tower, and, methinks, the four huge elms
Clustering, which mark the mansion of my friend;
And close behind them, hidden from my view,
Is my own lowly cottage, where my babe   225
And my babe's mother dwell in peace! With light
And quickened footsteps thitherward I tend,
Remembering thee, O green and silent dell!
And grateful, that by nature's quietness
And solitary musings, all my heart   230
Is softened, and made worthy to indulge
Love, and the thoughts that yearn for human kind.

(NETHER STOWEY, April 20, 1798)

GLOSSARY

dell – a small, secluded valley.
gay – here, 'bright'.
furze – an evergreen shrub with rudimentary leaves and yellow
   flowers.
flax – a food and fibre crop cultivated in cooler regions of the
   world.
fain – gladly.
Cairo – In 1798, Napoleon led the French army into Egypt,
   swiftly conquering Alexandria and Cairo.
perdition – a state of eternal punishment. Hell.
Book of Life – The Bible.
perjury – lying while under oath.

athwart – across.

phraseman – writer.

gored – a small to medium size perennial herbaceous plant of the buttercup family.

burthen – unburden.

amities – friendships.

fancy-points – a design in lace.

drudges – people made to do hard menial work.

my friend – Thomas Poole (1766–1837).

babe – his first son, Hartley Coleridge (1796-1849).

Nether Stowey – a village in Somerset, South West England. It sits in the foothills of the Quantock Hills. Coleridge lived near here from 1797 to 1799.

QUESTIONS

The poem is written in blank verse (unrhymed iambic pentameter). Select any four lines and underline the stressed an unstressed syllables.

This poem is classified as one of Coleridge's "conversation poems". On the other hand, Dowden) described it as "rather a sort of middle thing between Poetry and Oratory". Pick out sections of the poem which are like oratory (a speech).

How does Coleridge describe Nature in the first strophe? Comment on effective adjectives, use of alliteration, and his Pantheistic beliefs.

What change of tone is signalled by the opening line of the second strophe? Make a list of the things that are making him "melancholy", then examine how he presents his ideas and arguments.

Rewite this section (lines 29-29) in blank verse, free verse or prose, referring to the political problems in Britain today? Comment on the similarities and differences. Alternatively you could rewrite it as a conversation in which you meet the ghost of Coleridge and compare and contrast the politics of our time and his.

What arguments does Coleridge give against war? Which do you find the most powerful?

Coleridge originally supported the French Revolution. What does he think of the French at the time of writing this poem? What are the reasons for his change of heart?

What "bitter truth" does Coleridge want to communicate?

Describe the emotions expressed in the homecoming scene in the last strophe.

How does these intimate and tender emotions put his political opinions in perspective?

Choose three words to describe the tone of this poem. Justify your choice of words with reference to the text.

Critics have not been kind to the poem (for example, Swinburne, Dowden, Radley) and several think that it is rambling and lacking in focus. Do you agree, or do you think the Nature-Politics-Nature structure is effective?

COMMENTARY

This poem could be described as a Nature-Politics-Nature sandwich. The master stroke of the poem is that placing political concerns in the context of a religious view of the beauty of Nature, gives them an added poignancy.

Coleridge begins by describing a beautiful place in the Quantock Hills in Somerset. It is "green and silent", except for the lark's "minstrelsy". Alliterating adjectives like, "gay", "gorgeous" and "golden" describe the furze. The sunshine, continuing the alliterative adjectives, "glimmers". He then goes on to express some of his Pantheistic beliefs: it is a "spirit-healing nook", with "sweet influences" and "religious meanings". He describes an imaginary person in "early manhood" (someone like himself) who is subject to these influences and "dreams of better worlds".

The tone changes in the next strophe with an impassioned outcry at the threat to peace: "My God!", repeated a few lines later. He goes on to discuss the politics of the war in France and its implications. It is, in some respects like a political pamphlet and was first published as such in 1798. It has been described (by Dowden) as "rather a sort of middle thing between Poetry and Oratory". We note in lines 31/32 his concern "for all his human brethren". He explains that he sees this threat to peace as divine retribution ("We have offended very grievously!"). That offence is what the French have done in Cairo, and also what the British have done through imperialism:

> Even so, my countrymen! have we gone forth
> And borne to distant tribes slavery and pangs,
> And, deadlier far, our vices, whose deep taint
> With slow perdition murders the whole man,
> His body and his soul!

He goes on to complain of abuses at home. These include:

- The ineffectiveness and hypocrisy of "Courts, Committees, Institutions,/ Associations and Societies", which he attributes to "Pollutions from the brimming cup of wealth". Which has the effect of "bartering freedom and the poor man's life/ For gold, as at a market!"

- Abuses in the Christian church, including poor preaching, The Bible used as a "superstitious instrument", as a guarantor of the oaths which were sworn upon it.

- An attack on Atheism, which he does with a powerful extended metaphor: "the owlet Atheism,/ Sailing on obscene wings athwart the noon" etc.

- War-mongering amongst those who are "ignorant of all/ Its ghastlier workings".

Coleridge was a radical, and formerly, a Jacobin (a **Jacobin** is member of a radical political group, especially a group advocating egalitarian democracy and engaging in revolutionary activities) who was opposed to the British government under prime minister William Pitt. However, these criticisms are vague and generalised – though readers at the time may have been aware of specific instances of the abuses he describes. On the other hand, their very generality makes them more universal. For example, there is much that he says that could be applied to British politics in the 21st century.

Many of his points are supported by eloquent arguments, in particular against war (he is referring specifically to colonial wars, but is also points out that "retributive providence" might bring these horrors to Britain). One of his most powerful arguments refers to the general public's lack of understanding of what it is like to die in battle:

> We join no feeling and attach no form!
> As if the soldier died without a wound...

He paints a vivid picture of what it would be like if the British had to suffer invasion:

> Oh! let not English women drag their flight
> Fainting beneath the burthen of their babes,
> Of the sweet infants, that but yesterday
> Laughed at the breast!

He urges British men to "repel an impious foe", and goes on to be highly critical of the French:

> Who laugh away all virtue, mingling mirth
> With deeds of murder; and still promising
> Freedom, themselves too sensual to be free...

Coleridge was a Jacobin and had supported the revolution, but turned against it when it lost its original ideals and turned into a bloodbath. He opposed Napoleon's imperialistic campaigns (he was also opposed to British imperialism). There is, perhaps, some contradiction in his urging the British to fight the French foe, when he has previously expressed himself so eloquently against war. However, there is a big difference between unnecessary colonial wars and "fighting for survival" (to quote Bob Marley).

The next strophe is a repudiation of Jacobin views (views that he once held himself). He begins by warning the reader that he is going to state "a bitter truth", and that truth is that revolution to establish an egalitarian democracy is a "deep delusion". He uses an imaginative simile to explain that constitutional power is more than an outward show, "Like fancy-points and fringes, with the robe/ Pulled off at pleasure." He admits in the next that he once believed that: "Such have I been deemed." The strophe continues with a kind of apology in an apostrophe to his country, "O dear Britain!" He goes on to enumerate all that he owes to the "Mother Isle", which is, in the main, a list of natural beauty such as, "Lakes and mountain hills,/ thy clouds, they quiet dales, thy rocks and seas..." which have given him "All sweet sensations, all ennobling thoughts..." Coleridge's Pantheism reaches its height when he describes the country as a "most magnificent temple".

In the final strophe, he turns from Britain in general to his "soft and silent spot" where evening is approaching. There is more beautiful nature description: "the ivied beacon", "the green sheep-track" and the "heathy hill". As he approaches home, he describes it with the metaphor "huge amphitheatre of rich/ And elmy fields." Note how the noun 'elm', is here transformed into an adjective. He refers now to familiar things: "beloved Stowey", the "church-tower" and "the mansion of my friend" – and home itself: "my own lowly cottage" and his "babe" and wife. He ends by expressing the sense of gratitude he feels, for Nature and its effect on him, and the love he feels for all "human kind."

FROST AT MIDNIGHT

The Frost performs its secret ministry,
Unhelped by any wind. The owlet's cry
Came loud—and hark, again! loud as before.
The inmates of my cottage, all at rest,
Have left me to that solitude, which suits
Abstruser musings: save that at my side
My cradled infant slumbers peacefully.
'Tis calm indeed! so calm that it disturbs
And vexes meditation with its strange
And extreme silentness. Sea, hill, and wood,
This populous village! Sea, and hill, and wood,
With all the numberless goings-on of life,
Inaudible as dreams! the thin blue flame
Lies on my low-burnt fire, and quivers not;
Only that film, which fluttered on the grate,
Still flutters there, the sole unquiet thing.
Methinks, its motion in this hush of nature
Gives it dim sympathies with me who live,
Making it a companionable form,
Whose puny flaps and freaks the idling Spirit
By its own moods interprets, every where
Echo or mirror seeking of itself,
And makes a toy of Thought.

But O! how oft,

How oft, at school, with most believing mind,
Presageful, have I gazed upon the bars,   25
To watch that fluttering *stranger*! and as oft
With unclosed lids, already had I dreamt
Of my sweet birth-place, and the old church-tower,
Whose bells, the poor man's only music, rang
From morn to evening, all the hot Fair-day,   30
So sweetly, that they stirred and haunted me
With a wild pleasure, falling on mine ear
Most like articulate sounds of things to come!
So gazed I, till the soothing things, I dreamt,
Lulled me to sleep, and sleep prolonged my dreams!   35
And so I brooded all the following morn,
Awed by the stern preceptor's face, mine eye
Fixed with mock study on my swimming book:
Save if the door half opened, and I snatched
A hasty glance, and still my heart leaped up,   40
For still I hoped to see the *stranger's* face,
Townsman, or aunt, or sister more beloved,
My play-mate when we both were clothed alike!

   Dear Babe, that sleepest cradled by my side,
Whose gentle breathings, heard in this deep calm,   45
Fill up the interspersèd vacancies
And momentary pauses of the thought!
My babe so beautiful! it thrills my heart
With tender gladness, thus to look at thee,
And think that thou shalt learn far other lore,   50
And in far other scenes! For I was reared
In the great city, pent 'mid cloisters dim,
And saw nought lovely but the sky and stars.
But *thou*, my babe! shalt wander like a breeze
By lakes and sandy shores, beneath the crags   55
Of ancient mountain, and beneath the clouds,
Which image in their bulk both lakes and shores
And mountain crags: so shalt thou see and hear
The lovely shapes and sounds intelligible
Of that eternal language, which thy God   60
Utters, who from eternity doth teach
Himself in all, and all things in himself.

Great universal Teacher! he shall mould
Thy spirit, and by giving make it ask.

Therefore all seasons shall be sweet to thee, 65
Whether the summer clothe the general earth
With greenness, or the redbreast sit and sing
Betwixt the tufts of snow on the bare branch
Of mossy apple-tree, while the nigh thatch
Smokes in the sun-thaw; whether the eave-drops fall 70
Heard only in the trances of the blast,
Or if the secret ministry of frost
Shall hang them up in silent icicles,
Quietly shining to the quiet Moon.

(February, 1798)

GLOSSARY

abstruser – comparative of 'abstruse' – difficult to understand, in other words, his solitude is suitable for more complex thoughts.

infant –his first son, Hartley Coleridge (1796-1849).

thin blue flame – these flames were called 'strangers' and were believed to predict the arrival of an absent friend.

school – Christ's Hospital, a charity school in Greyfriars, London.

birth-place – Ottery St Mary in Devon.

preceptor – here, 'teacher'.

lore – traditional knowledge or belief.

pent – here, 'held in'.

cloisters – a covered passage on the side of a court.

crags – steep rugged cliffs.

eave-drops – drops of water from the eaves (edges) of the roof.

QUESTIONS

This is one of Coleridge's most successful "conversation poems". Pick out words and phrases that have a conversational tone. Also, analyse a selection of lines in terms of syllable count and stress count. Look for enjambment and repetition, then describe how Coleridge manages to sustain the effect of conversation within the metre of blank verse.

How does Coleridge express his surprise at the extreme silence?

What does the blue flame in the fire represent in popular mythology and how does it influence Coleridge's train of thought?

How do we know (from this poem) that Coleridge's schooldays were unhappy?

What kind of an education does he plan for his son?

What does he believe the effect of Nature will be on his son?

What evidence is there in this poem of Coleridge's Pantheism? (Pantheism: a doctrine which identifies God with the universe, or regards the universe as a manifestation of God).

Write a short gloss for each strophe (similar to the glosses in *The Ancient Mariner*) saying what each strophe is about. Give each strophe a heading.

The last strophe contains a "return" - a common feature of the structure of Coleridge's poems. Explain what this is and examine its effect.

Choose three words to describe the tone of this poem. Justify your choice of words with reference to the text.

Turn this poem into a real conversation by the interpolation of responses (in free verse, blank verse, or prose) about your own education and your beliefs about what an ideal education would be like.

COMMENTARY

The word 'ministry' in the first line is interesting because the base meaning of the word is: the service of a minister of religion, though it can mean, in a more general sense: something that serves as an agency. The capitalisation of 'Frost' suggests personification, but the pronoun 'its' undermines that impression, and nowhere else in the poem is there any hint of the personification of 'Frost'. However, the word 'ministry' does suggest some kind of religious agency, which is in keeping with Coleridge's Pantheistic view of nature. The purpose of the frost and the "owlet's cry" is to create a sense of "solitude", which facilitates his "abstruser musings". The infant Hartley is with him, but sleeping quietly. He is amazed at the "extreme silentness". He enumerates what is around him: "this populous village! Sea, and hill, and wood" to emphasise his surprise at the silence. He describes it with a telling simile: "inaudible as dreams". In other words, the situation has a dreamlike quality (has he been at the opium again?). He goes on to describe one of the key symbols in the poem, "the thin blue flame" in the "low-burnt fire". Those of us who can remember living with coal fires will remember this phenomenon, which is caused by methane gas. In popular mythology, these flames were called "strangers" and were believed to predict the arrival of an absent friend, and this makes the flame seem "companionable". Indeed, it is personified with the words "by its own moods" and interacts with the poet by interrupting his "abstruser musings" as it "makes a toy of Thought.".

The blue flame takes him back to his schooldays where he recalls watching a similar "stranger" which soothes his homesickness for "my sweet birth-place". He does not seem happy at school. His teacher is "stern" and he can only pretend to study. The phrase "swimming book" suggests that there are tears in his eyes, but the thought that a "stranger" is coming helps him to bear up. Indeed, every time the door opens, he hopes to see a familiar face.

Memories of his unhappy youth makes his thoughts turn to his "babe" ('baby' - not a hot girlfriend) and express the hope that he shall "learn far other lore", in other words, have a different kind of education, the word "lore" suggesting that it will be based on more traditional beliefs (in this case, a belief in the power of Nature). He enumerates the natural phenomena that Harley will benefit from:

But *thou*, my babe! shalt wander like a breeze
By lakes and sandy shores, beneath the crags
Of ancient mountain, and beneath the clouds...

Coleridge continues by explaining why it is so important: it is the "eternal language, which thy God/ Utters". His Pantheism is very clearly stated in the next line: "Himself in all, and all things in himself" (this is, indeed, close to the dictionary definition of Pantheism.) Coleridge expresses the hope that this "Great universal Teacher!" will "mould" his son's spirit. Coleridge had a sincere belief in the beneficial effects of Nature, but it seems that this alternative education did not work out as Coleridge had hoped. Hartley's brother, Derwent says this about Hartley's time at Greta Hall:

"The unlimited indulgence with which he was treated at Greta Hall, tended, without doubt, to strengthen the many and strong peculiarities of his nature, and may perhaps have contributed to that waywardness and want of control, from which in later-life he suffered so deeply."

The final strophe is the "return" which is a noted feature of Coleridge's conversation poems. Having begin with "abstruser musings" we have followed his train of thought from the blue flames of the fire, to his memories of his unhappy schooldays and his plans to give his "babe" a better kind of education, then back again to the "secret ministry of frost". The strophe ends with a sense of stillness and beauty, which mirrors the stillness and beauty of the opening and gives a sense of closure to his troubled (unhappy memories) and impassioned (opinions about the beneficial effect of Nature) train of thought.

DEJECTION: AN ODE

Late, late yestreen I saw the new Moon,
With the old Moon in her arms;
And I fear, I fear, my Master dear!
We shall have a deadly storm.
Ballad of Sir Patrick Spence

I

Well! If the Bard was weather-wise, who made
  The grand old ballad of Sir Patrick Spence,
  This night, so tranquil now, will not go hence
Unroused by winds, that ply a busier trade
Than those which mould yon cloud in lazy flakes,   5
Or the dull sobbing draft, that moans and rakes
Upon the strings of this Æolian lute,
  Which better far were mute.
  For lo! the New-moon winter-bright!
  And overspread with phantom light,   10
  (With swimming phantom light o'erspread
  But rimmed and circled by a silver thread)
I see the old Moon in her lap, foretelling
  The coming-on of rain and squally blast.
And oh! that even now the gust were swelling,   15
  And the slant night-shower driving loud and fast!
Those sounds which oft have raised me, whilst they awed,

> And sent my soul abroad,
> Might now perhaps their wonted impulse give,
> Might startle this dull pain, and make it move and live!　　　20

II

> A grief without a pang, void, dark, and drear,
> 　A stifled, drowsy, unimpassioned grief,
> 　Which finds no natural outlet, no relief,
> 　　In word, or sigh, or tear–
> O Lady! in this wan and heartless mood,　　　25
> To other thoughts by yonder throstle woo'd,
> 　All this long eve, so balmy and serene,
> Have I been gazing on the western sky,
> 　And its peculiar tint of yellow green:
> And still I gaze–and with how blank an eye!　　　30
> And those thin clouds above, in flakes and bars,
> That give away their motion to the stars;
> Those stars, that glide behind them or between,
> Now sparkling, now bedimmed, but always seen:
> Yon crescent Moon, as fixed as if it grew　　　35
> In its own cloudless, starless lake of blue;
> I see them all so excellently fair,
> I see, not feel, how beautiful they are!

III

> 　My genial spirits fail;
> 　And what can these avail　　　40
> To lift the smothering weight from off my breast?
> 　It were a vain endeavour,
> 　Though I should gaze for ever
> On that green light that lingers in the west:
> I may not hope from outward forms to win　　　45
> The passion and the Life, whose fountains are within.

IV

> O Lady! we receive but what we give,
> And in our life alone does Nature live:

Ours is her wedding garment, ours her shroud!
  And would we aught behold, of higher worth,   50
Than that inanimate cold world allowed
To the poor loveless ever-anxious crowd,
  Ah! from the soul itself must issue forth
A light, a glory, a fair luminous cloud
    Enveloping the Earth—   55
And from the soul itself must there be sent
  A sweet and potent voice, of its own birth,
Of all sweet sounds the life and element!

V

O pure of heart! thou need'st not ask of me
What this strong music in the soul may be!   60
What, and wherein it doth exist,
This light, this glory, this fair luminous mist,
This beautiful and beauty-making power.
  Joy, virtuous Lady! Joy that ne'er was given,
Save to the pure, and in their purest hour,   65
Life, and Life's effluence, cloud at once and shower,
Joy, Lady! is the spirit and the power,
Which wedding Nature to us gives in dower
  A new Earth and new Heaven,
Undreamt of by the sensual and the proud—   70
Joy is the sweet voice, Joy the luminous cloud—
    We in ourselves rejoice!
And thence flows all that charms or ear or sight,
  All melodies the echoes of that voice,
All colours a suffusion from that light.   75

VI

There was a time when, though my path was rough,
  This joy within me dallied with distress,
And all misfortunes were but as the stuff
  Whence Fancy made me dreams of happiness:
For hope grew round me, like the twining vine,   80
And fruits, and foliage, not my own, seemed mine.
But now afflictions bow me down to earth:

143

Nor care I that they rob me of my mirth;
  But oh! each visitation
Suspends what nature gave me at my birth,   85
  My shaping spirit of Imagination.
For not to think of what I needs must feel,
  But to be still and patient, all I can;
And haply by abstruse research to steal
  From my own nature all the natural man—   90
  This was my sole resource, my only plan:
Till that which suits a part infects the whole,
And now is almost grown the habit of my soul.

VII

Hence, viper thoughts, that coil around my mind,
  Reality's dark dream!   95
I turn from you, and listen to the wind,
  Which long has raved unnoticed. What a scream
Of agony by torture lengthened out
That lute sent forth! Thou Wind, that rav'st without,
  Bare crag, or mountain-tairn,[367:1] or blasted tree,   100
Or pine-grove whither woodman never clomb,
Or lonely house, long held the witches' home,
  Methinks were fitter instruments for thee,
Mad Lutanist! who in this month of showers,
Of dark-brown gardens, and of peeping flowers,   105
Mak'st Devils' yule, with worse than wintry song,
The blossoms, buds, and timorous leaves among.
  Thou Actor, perfect in all tragic sounds!
Thou mighty Poet, e'en to frenzy bold!
  What tell'st thou now about?   110
  'Tis of the rushing of an host in rout,
  With groans, of trampled men, with smarting wounds—
At once they groan with pain, and shudder with the cold!
But hush! there is a pause of deepest silence!
  And all that noise, as of a rushing crowd,   115
With groans, and tremulous shudderings—all is over—
  It tells another tale, with sounds less deep and loud!
  A tale, of less affright,
  And tempered with delight,

As Otway's self had framed the tender lay,–   120
   'Tis of a little child
   Upon a lonesome wild,
Not far from home, but she hath lost her way:
And now moans low in bitter grief and fear,
And now screams loud, and hopes to make her mother hear.

VIII

'Tis midnight, but small thoughts have I of sleep: 126
Full seldom may my friend such vigils keep!
Visit her, gentle Sleep! with wings of healing,
  And may this storm be but a mountain-birth,
May all the stars hang bright above her dwelling,   130
  Silent as though they watched the sleeping Earth!
   With light heart may she rise,
   Gay fancy, cheerful eyes,
  Joy lift her spirit, joy attune her voice;
To her may all things live, from pole to pole,   135
Their life the eddying of her living soul!
  O simple spirit, guided from above,
Dear Lady! friend devoutest of my choice,
Thus mayest thou ever, evermore rejoice.

(1802)

GLOSSARY

yestreen – yesterday evening.
ply – to work at diligently.
Aeolian lute – his Aeolian harp, here called 'Aeolian lute' to
  rhyme with 'mute'.
squally – a squall is a sudden, violet gust of wind.
wonted – accustomed.
pang – a sudden feeling of mental or emotional distress or
  longing.
yonder/yon – over there.
throstle – a poetic word for 'thrush'.
aught – anything.

effluence – a substance that flows out from something.
suffusion – steep rugged cliffs.
Fancy – a personification of imagination.
ravs't – archaic second person of 'rave'.
tairn – the Scottish spelling of 'tarn', a mountain lake.
clomb – archaic past tense of 'climb'.
Devil's yule – an alternative Christmas ceremony presided over by the demon, Krampus. 'Yule' was the name of the Nordic pre-Christian mid-winter celebration.
timorous – fearful.
rout – a defeat with disorderly flight.
Otway – Thomas Otway, (1652 –1685) an English playwright who was popular at the time.
vigil – a period of keeping awake during the time usually spent asleep, especially to keep watch or pray.
gay fancy – bright and cheerful imagination.

QUESTIONS

Analyse the verse form of the first strophe. Look for iambic pentameters, tetrameters and an alexandrine. Do the same with strophe III.

How does Coleridge describe the storm? How does he link it to his mood of dejection?

In strophe II, what words and images does he use to describe his dejection in detail?

What words and images does he use to describe nature in this strophe? What regret does he express in the last two lines?

In strophe III, he expresses his growing understanding that "passion and life" do not come from "outward forms". Where do they come from?

How does he expand this idea in strophe IV, and what language does he use to express it? How does this language compare with that used by Wordsworth in *Ode: Intimations of Immortality from*

Recollections of Early Childhood (read the first two strophes, or at least read the example on page 12-13).

What does Coleridge say about the importance of joy in strophe V?

In strophe VI, what does Coleridge say about the effect of dejection on his creative powers?

Analyse in detail how Coleridge personifies the wind in strophe VII. Point out the elements of the sublime and the gothic.

What stories does he imagine the "poet-wind" to be telling in this strophe?

How does strophe VIII round off the poem? Is there a sense of return? What good wishes does he send to Sara?

Choose three words to describe the tone of this poem. Justify your choice of words with reference to the text.

COMMENTARY

In 1799 Coleridge and his wife Sara moved to Greta Hall, Keswick. Coleridge spent a great deal of time with Wordsworth and fell in love with his wife's sister, Sara Hutchinson. She did not encourage his advances, but he became obsessed with her, and was estranged from his wife, whom he blamed for all his troubles. *Dejection* was first written as a verse letter entitled *Letter to Sara Hutchinson*, but when he came to publish it in 1802, he omitted many of the most personal passages, resulting a poem of about one third the length of the original that is, in the words of George Watson (1966), "to be preferred as a finished work of art."

This poem is a Pindaric Ode (the form is named after the Greek poet Pindar, c. 522 – c. 443 BC, though the form of his odes is different). A Pindaric Ode consists of a series of stanzas which are irregular in form, having different metrical patterns and rhyme schemes. In the ode, Coleridge mixes iambic pentameters with tetrameters and the occasional alexandrine, and uses a variable rhyme scheme.

The first stanza refers to the weather-lore in *The Ballad of Sir Patrick Spence,* which he quotes as an epigraph. This is one of the most popular of British traditional ballads, first published in 1765 in Bishop Thomas Percy's *Reliques of Ancient English Poetry.* It shows the kind of poetry that Coleridge enjoyed reading, and which influenced his style. He describes similar signs in the weather outside in richly poetic terms containing a touch of personification and a vivid metaphor:

> (With swimming phantom light o'erspread
> But rimmed and circled by a silver thread)

He goes on to describe the storm building up and expresses the hope that it might "startle" him out of his dejection, and inspire him, as such storms have inspired him before.

He begins the next strophe by describing his dejection as fully as possible. The phrase "grief without a pang" tells us that it is long and drawn out, but without any sudden feelings of anguish that might, perhaps, have jolted him out of it. This is followed by a series of adjectives for the word "grief": "void, dark, and drear...stifled, drowsy, unimpassioned". The words "stifled" and "drowsy" suggest that he has being trying to cure it with opium. The strophe continues with an address to Sarah Hutchinson ("O Lady!"), though in this edited version for publication, she is not named. He tells her how he has been contemplating the beauties of nature, particularly a "peculiar tint of yellow green" in the evening sky, and stars, described with perceptive detail as "now sparkling, now bedimmed". He describes the moon metaphorically as floating in a "starless lake of blue". Then he laments that, though he sees these beauties, his dejection prevents him from responding emotionally: "I see, not feel, how beautiful they are!"

He continues this lament in the next strophe and ends by making the point that "outward forms" cannot give "life and "passion", because they can only come from "within". In other words, only a sense of requited love could awake his emotions, and enable him to respond to nature.

Coleridge begins Strophe IV by addressing Sara again, though instead of love talk, he gives her some of his Pantheistic philosophy. He says that Nature only lives through human life, and without that it is an "inanimate cold world". Anything of "higher worth" (he is probably referring to spiritual values) comes from the human soul. He reinforces this point with a powerful image:

> A light, a glory, a fair luminous cloud
>   Enveloping the Earth—

This perhaps owes something to the inspiration of Wordsworth's Ode: *Intimations of Immortality from Recollections of Early Childhood*:

> There was a time when meadow, grove, and stream,
> The earth, and every common sight,
> To me did seem
> Apparelled in celestial light...

In Strophe V, Coleridge, continuing to address Sara ("O pure of heart!") says what this quality, described metaphorically as "strong music", is: it is "Joy", (the word "Love" would have made more sense in view of his feelings for Sara. Perhaps he is hinting this.) He continues in the ecstatic language of the previous strophe (in imitation of Wordsworth). He describes Joy with metaphors: "sweet voice" and "luminous cloud", and asserts that everything we see or hear come from, in another metaphor, "that light".

In the next strophe Coleridge relates how, in the past, he felt joy mixed with despair, and his imagination was able to make him happy (no doubt, by inspiring poetry). This caused him to be hopeful. He describes hope with a powerful, extended simile of a vine. The "fruits, and foliage" are poems which grew out of it. He goes on to say that he does not feel this now, and laments that his "Imagination" is suspended. It is interesting that in this line, he expresses something that creative artists often feel — that his best work is "not my own". He feels that his dejection is robbing him of the imaginative power to produce such work (though, ironically, he is in process of producing one of his best) but hopes that "abstruse research" may compensate for this to some extent. He is perhaps referring to his prose works.

Strophe VII is, in the editor's opinion, the finest part of the poem. It begins with the striking metaphor, "viper thoughts", which vividly convey how these dejected thoughts poison his mind. The oxymoron tacked onto the end of this sentence is even more powerful. The poisonous thoughts are "reality", but they are not real because they are a "dark dream". This suggest that reality is not real at all – it is the life of the imagination that is real. This is a form of Platonic philosophy that is hinted at, but not developed, because he wants to get it out of his mind. To achieve this, he listens to the wind which is personified at length. He is describing the sound of the wind in his Aeolian harp (which, to be consistent with line 7, he continues to call "Aeolian lute"). It is a "scream / Of agony by torture lengthened out". He goes on to imagine a scene of wild nature that is a textbook example of the sublime. (The personification of the wind culminates in the phrase "Mad Lutanist! (referring to the way it is playing his Aeolian harp). The sublime begins to merge into the gothic (which takes the idea of the sublime to its most extreme form). The first hint of gothic was "the witches' home", but he goes on to describe the Devil's Yule as an image to describe the screaming wind. read the note in the glossary and you will see that this a very extreme image. However, Coleridge goes on by varying the personification of the wind to emphasise more positive qualities. It is an "Actor" (though tragic), and a "Poet" (though with an emphasis on "frenzy"). From line 110 he speculates about the tales that the wind-poet tells. His first thought is about the "rout" of an army, then silence, then a "rushing crowd", then a tale which reminds him of Otway's plays (perhaps *The Orphan*) of "a little child/ Upon a lonesome wild" who has lost her way and his crying for her mother. A tragic image – but it is only something he imagines in the wind – not real.

In the last strophe there is a return to a calmer mood. Coleridge says that, though he will not be able to sleep (he expresses his problems with sleep in *The Pains of Sleep*) he addresses Sleep (a personification) and asks her to "visit" Sara. He continues with the wish that she will rise refreshed and experience "joy". The poem ends with a dedication to her "friend devoutest of my choice", and a wish for her lasting happiness.

THE PAINS OF SLEEP

Ere on my bed my limbs I lay,
It hath not been my use to pray
With moving lips or bended knees;
But silently, by slow degrees,
My spirit I to Love compose,   5
In humble trust mine eye-lids close,
With reverential resignation,
No wish conceived, no thought exprest,
Only a sense of supplication;
A sense o'er all my soul imprest   10
That I am weak, yet not unblest,
Since in me, round me, every where
Eternal Strength and Wisdom are.

But yester-night I prayed aloud
In anguish and in agony,   15
Up-starting from the fiendish crowd
Of shapes and thoughts that tortured me:
A lurid light, a trampling throng,
Sense of intolerable wrong,
And whom I scorned, those only strong!   20
Thirst of revenge, the powerless will
Still baffled, and yet burning still!
Desire with loathing strangely mixed
On wild or hateful objects fixed.

Fantastic passions! maddening brawl!   25
And shame and terror over all!
Deeds to be hid which were not hid,
Which all confused I could not know
Whether I suffered, or I did:
For all seemed guilt, remorse or woe,   30
My own or others still the same
Life-stifling fear, soul-stifling shame.

So two nights passed: the night's dismay
Saddened and stunned the coming day.
Sleep, the wide blessing, seemed to me   35
Distemper's worst calamity.
The third night, when my own loud scream
Had waked me from the fiendish dream,
O'ercome with sufferings strange and wild,
I wept as I had been a child;   40
And having thus by tears subdued
My anguish to a milder mood,
Such punishments, I said, were due
To natures deepliest stained with sin,–
For aye entempesting anew   45
The unfathomable hell within,
The horror of their deeds to view,
To know and loathe, yet wish and do!
Such griefs with such men well agree,
But wherefore, wherefore fall on me?   50
To be beloved is all I need,
And whom I love, I love indeed.

(1803)

GLOSSARY

ere – before (poetic).
supplication – asking for something earnestly and humbly.
throng – crowd.
brawl – a rough, noisy fight.
distempter – here, illness.

aye – forever (poetic).
entempesting – making a storm (poetic).
unfathomable – cannot be fully understood.

QUESTIONS

Analyse the rhyme and metre of the first strophe and compare
Compare it with the more leisurely, unrhymed iambic pentameters
conversations poems. How is the verse form of this poem suited to
the subject-matter?

Describe Coleridge's usual routine when going to bed. What
does he say about prayer?

What words, phrases and imagery does Coleridge use to convey
an impression of the nightmares he experienced?

Explain the meaning and the power of the compound adjectives
"life-stifling" and "soul-stifling" in the last lines of Strophe II.

What words and phrases in Strophe III show the depths of his
suffering?

Research Coleridge's earlier experience of nightmares.

Research withdrawal symptoms and consider whether the
symptoms described in this poem arise from his attempt to control
his opium addiction.

What does he think is the reason for his suffering? Apart from
opium addiction, what other things has Coleridge done wrong in
his life?

Discuss the last two lines in the light of what you know of his
private life. How far are the lines justified?

Choose three words to describe the tone of this poem. Justify
your choice of words with reference to the text.

COMMENTARY

The poem is written in tetrameters with a variable rhyme scheme, mainly couplets. which have a very different effect to the blank verse of his conversation poems. The shorter lines, clinched with rhyme, give an effect of terseness and urgency which is appropriate to the subject-matter.

Coleridge begins by describing how he usually goes to bed and goes to sleep. He explains that he does not pray in the conventional sense of the word, but composes his spirit in a "reverential" manner. He does not make any wishes or express any thoughts, but nevertheless has a "sense of supplication". He feels that he is "weak" but that there is "Eternal Strength and Wisdom" all around him, and this is what he is unconsciously asking for.

He is leading up to a description of his suffering the night before, when he "prayed aloud in "anguish and agony" after waking up from a "fiendish crowd/ Of shapes and thoughts that tortured me." He experienced a mixture of powerful emotions ("fantastic passions"): a "sense of intolerable wrong", "scorn,", "thirst of revenge", "bafflement", "desire", "loathing", "shame", "terror", "guilt", "remorse", "woe". "fear". These emotions were aroused by "wild or hateful objects". Shameful things were done which should be hidden, but were not, and everything was very "confused": "I could now know/ Whether I suffered, or I did." Coleridge's nightmares predated his addiction to opium, though the nightmare's in this poem sound very like a description of withdrawal symptoms. As poetry, it is very powerful because of the intensity of the description, in which emotions are piled one on another in a way that almost makes the reader share Coleridge's experience.

Coleridge tells us that he suffered for two nights in this way, and that sleep, "the wide blessing" became the worse thing about his "distemper" (illness). The third night is the worst. He is "O'ercome with sufferings strange and wild," and sees it as Divine punishment for "sin" (taking opium, and perhaps his neglect of his wife and family). The metaphor of hell tells us how much he suffered. The last lines are almost self-pitying:

To be beloved is all I need,
And whom I love, I love indeed.

and in view of the way he treated his wife, demonstrably untrue.

TO WILLIAM WORDSWORTH

COMPOSED ON THE NIGHT AFTER HIS RECITATION OF A POEM ON THE GROWTH OF AN INDIVIDUAL MIND

Friend of the wise! and Teacher of the Good!
Into my heart have I received that Lay
More than historic, that prophetic Lay
Wherein (high theme by thee first sung aright)
Of the foundations and the building up   5
Of a Human Spirit thou hast dared to tell
What may be told, to the understanding mind
Revealable; and what within the mind
By vital breathings secret as the soul
Of vernal growth, oft quickens in the heart   10
Thoughts all too deep for words!–
                Theme hard as high!
Of smiles spontaneous, and mysterious fears
(The first-born they of Reason and twin-birth),
Of tides obedient to external force,
And currents self-determined, as might seem,   15
Or by some inner Power; of moments awful,
Now in thy inner life, and now abroad,
When power streamed from thee, and thy soul received
The light reflected, as a light bestowed–
Of fancies fair, and milder hours of youth,   20
Hyblean murmurs of poetic thought

Industrious in its joy, in vales and glens
Native or outland, lakes and famous hills!
Or on the lonely high-road, when the stars
Were rising; or by secret mountain-streams,   25
The guides and the companions of thy way!

Of more than Fancy, of the Social Sense
Distending wide, and man beloved as man,
Where France in all her towns lay vibrating
Like some becalmèd bark beneath the burst   30
Of Heaven's immediate thunder, when no cloud
Is visible, or shadow on the main.
For thou wert there, thine own brows garlanded,
Amid the tremor of a realm aglow,
Amid a mighty nation jubilant,   35
When from the general heart of human kind
Hope sprang forth like a full-born Deity!
—Of that dear Hope afflicted and struck down,
So summoned homeward, thenceforth calm and sure
From the dread watch-tower of man's absolute self,   40
With light unwaning on her eyes, to look
Far on—herself a glory to behold,
The Angel of the vision! Then (last strain)
Of Duty, chosen Laws controlling choice,
Action and joy!–An Orphic song indeed,   45
A song divine of high and passionate thoughts
To their own music chaunted!

        O great Bard!
Ere yet that last strain dying awed the air,
With stedfast eye I viewed thee in the choir
Of ever-enduring men. The truly great   50
Have all one age, and from one visible space
Shed influence! They, both in power and act,
Are permanent, and Time is not with them,
Save as it worketh for them, they in it.
Nor less a sacred Roll, than those of old,   55
And to be placed, as they, with gradual fame
Among the archives of mankind, thy work
Makes audible a linkèd lay of Truth,

Of Truth profound a sweet continuous lay,
Not learnt, but native, her own natural notes!   60
Ah! as I listened with a heart forlorn,
The pulses of my being beat anew:
And even as Life returns upon the drowned,
Life's joy rekindling roused a throng of pains—
Keen pangs of Love, awakening as a babe   65
Turbulent, with an outcry in the heart;
And fears self-willed, that shunned the eye of Hope;
And Hope that scarce would know itself from Fear;
Sense of past Youth, and Manhood come in vain,
And Genius given, and Knowledge won in vain;   70
And all which I had culled in wood-walks wild,
And all which patient toil had reared, and all,
Commune with thee had opened out—but flowers
Strewed on my corse, and borne upon my bier,
In the same coffin, for the self-same grave!   75

   That way no more! and ill beseems it me,
Who came a welcomer in herald's guise,
Singing of Glory, and Futurity,
To wander back on such unhealthful road,
Plucking the poisons of self-harm! And ill   80
Such intertwine beseems triumphal wreaths
Strew'd before thy advancing!

                Nor do thou,
Sage Bard! impair the memory of that hour
Of thy communion with my nobler mind
By pity or grief, already felt too long!   85
Nor let my words import more blame than needs.
The tumult rose and ceased: for Peace is nigh
Where Wisdom's voice has found a listening heart.
Amid the howl of more than wintry storms,
The Halcyon hears the voice of vernal hours   90
Already on the wing.

             Eve following eve,
Dear tranquil time, when the sweet sense of Home
Is sweetest! moments for their own sake hailed

And more desired, more precious, for thy song,
In silence listening, like a devout child,   95
My soul lay passive, by thy various strain
Driven as in surges now beneath the stars,
With momentary stars of my own birth,
Fair constellated foam,[408:1] still darting off
Into the darkness; now a tranquil sea,   100
Outspread and bright, yet swelling to the moon.

And when—O Friend! my comforter and guide!
Strong in thyself, and powerful to give strength!—
Thy long sustainéd Song finally closed,
And thy deep voice had ceased—yet thou thyself   105
Wert still before my eyes, and round us both
That happy vision of belovéd faces—
Scarce conscious, and yet conscious of its close
I sate, my being blended in one thought
(Thought was it? or aspiration? or resolve?)   110
Absorbed, yet hanging still upon the sound—
And when I rose, I found myself in prayer.

(January, 1807)

GLOSSARY

lay – a short narrative poem (though *The Prelude* is long, having
    14 books).
vernal – to do with Spring.
Hyblean – of Hybla, the name of a place in ancient Sicily that
    was renowned for its honey.
glen – a secluded and narrow valley.
outland – here, illness.
Fancy – forever (poetic).
distending – here, 'extending'.
bark – 'barque', a kind of sailing ship.
Orphic – relating to the mythical poet Orpheus. Apollo gave
    Orpheus a golden lyre, so he is often associated with music
    and poetry.
roll – a list of names.
forlorn – sad and lonely because of isolation or desertion.

corse – corpse.
bier – a coffin on a stand.
sage – wise.
Halcyon – (derived from Alcyone of Greek mythology)
    characterized by happiness, great success, and prosperity).

QUESTIONS

This poem is Coleridge's last successful "conversation poems", poems which are written in a conversational style. However, it is perhaps less informal, and contains more poetic diction than some of his earlier conversation poems. Analyse the metre of the first few lines, and make a list of poetic diction, e.g., "lay", "vernal", etc. (hint: several examples can be found in the glossary).

Despite the more formal style, it is nevertheless a deeply personal poem. Find and comment on these personal elements.

Read the first three strophes and say what Coleridge admired about Wordsworth's poem. What words, phrases and images does he use to describe it?

Explain the Pantheist philosophy that Coleridge describes in Wordsworth's poem.

What does Coleridge think the poem has done for Wordsworth's reputation as a poet?

In the next three strophes, what does Coleridge say about his own poetic endeavour? What images does he use to express his failure?

What positive feelings does this poem inspire in Coleridge? What words, phrases and images does he use to describe them?

If Coleridge had had more self-confidence, what might he have written in defence of his poetic achievements?

COMMENTARY

Wordsworth's *Prelude* is his most important work. The full title gives an idea what it is about: *The Prelude or, Growth of a Poet's Mind; An Autobiographical Poem.* In the poem, Wordsworth explores his relationship with Nature and explains how it help him to develop as a poet. Wordsworth read the poem aloud to Coleridge during the winter of 1806/1807, and *To William Wordsworth* is Coleridge's response.

The tone of awed admiration that characterises this poem is established in the opening lines: "Friend of the wise! and Teacher of the Good!" which praise Wordsworth as a great man. Coleridge goes to summarise the content of the poem. It is about "the building up/ Of a Human Spirit", which in Wordsworth's case, was a "vernal growth" (here, "vernal" is used more broadly to mean nature as a whole) and Wordsworth has expressed it in a very profound manner ("thoughts all too deep for words"). The growth of his spirit came from a combination of internal and external forces, and then expressed itself in poetry which Coleridge describes in an extended metaphor of light:

> When power streamed from thee, and thy soul received
> The light reflected, as a light bestowed—

He goes on to summarise some of the subject matter: Wordsworth's youth, when "vales and glens", "lakes and famous hills", and "mountain streams" were his "guides and companions".

The next strophe refers to Wordsworth's experiences in France, using the powerful extended image of a becalmed ship before the storm (the storm is, of course, the French Revolution in 1789). He describes in metaphorical terms the enthusiasm for the revolution in its early stages that he, Wordsworth, and many others felt at that time: "Hope sprang forth like a full-born Deity!" Disillusionment came in the bloody period of "The Terror", and Coleridge describes this by continuing his metaphor: "Hope afflicted and struck down". He tells how Wordsworth came back to England and began his "Orphic song" (*The Prelude*). The allusion is reinforced in the next line when Coleridge describes it as "a song divine".

The next strophe is the most interesting in the whole poem, as , instead of eulogising Wordsworth, he gives us an insight into his own thoughts and feelings. After praising Wordsworth as a "great Bard" who is "in the choir/ Of ever-enduring men" – in other words, has achieved immortality through the greatness of his poetry. He says that he listened with a "heart forlorn". The adjective is highly appropriate because it tells us that Coleridge feels lost and alone. Another word describing his mental state is used in line 63: "drowned". Again, a well-chosen word, because it describes metaphorically how his poetic powers has been affected by opium abuse. Wordsworth poem stirs something within him which he compares to "keen pangs of love" and "awakening as a babe...with an outcry in the heart" arising from his sense of his wasted opportunities. Youth and Manhood have "come in vain"; the "Genius" which he feels he was given, and the knowledge he has acquired, are also "in vain" (note the powerful repetition of that phrase. Also the influence of nature "culled in wood-walks wild", and of Wordsworth himself, has led to nothing – indeed, he describes it with the bitterest of extended metaphors:

> ...but flowers
> Strewed on my corse, and borne upon my bier,
> In the same coffin, for the self-same grave!

In the next stanza he attributes this failure to "the poisons of self-harm!", no doubt a reference to his opium addiction.

He softens these bitter thoughts somewhat in the next stanza, by saying that "Peace is nigh" because Wordsworth is a "listening heart" amid the "wintry storms" – a metaphor Coleridge often uses to describe his inner struggles.

The positive note continues in the next strophe. He describes the days of the reading of *The Prelude* as a "dear tranquil time". He refers to "momentary stars of my own birth" – a metaphor for his own poetry, including, perhaps, this one. He continues with another metaphor about his own poetry. He compares it to the foam in the sea and ends with a beautiful image of the sea at night:

> ...now a tranquil sea,
> Outspread and bright, yet swelling to the moon.

His final thoughts and feelings are admiration for his friend and a renewed sense of "aspiration" or "resolve" for his own poetic endeavour, the whole experience leaving him with a sense of religious fervour:

> And when I rose, I found myself in prayer.

This poem gives us an insight into the relationship between Coleridge and Wordsworth. Coleridge clearly idolises his friend, but denigrates himself. This was no doubt exacerbated by Coleridge's awareness of his inability to control his opium addiction, and the criticisms that Wordsworth had made of Coleridge's poems (for example, of the archaic diction in The Ancient Mariner). This is unfortunate, because although Wordsworth was revered in the nineteenth century, his reputation has declined in the twentieth and twenty-first centuries. At his best, his poetry, particularly the poetry of his "Great Decade" from 1798 to 1808, is innovative, inspired, elevated and philosophically profound, but at its worst, it is bombastic sententious, sentimental and narcissistic (see *The Egoism of Authorship: Wordsworth's Poetic Career*, Erickson, 1990). Coleridge, on the other hand, is also innovative, inspired, elevated and philosophically profound, but also, sincere, humble, and broader in scope, his main achievement being in the gothic genre with poems such as *The Ancient Mariner* and *Christabel*. Indeed, as time has passed, Wordsworth's critical reputation has declined, and Coleridge's has risen.

THE KNIGHT'S TOMB

Where is the grave of Sir Arthur O'Kellyn?
Where may the grave of that good man be?–
By the side of a spring, on the breast of Helvellyn,
Under the twigs of a young birch tree!
The oak that in summer was sweet to hear,   5
And rustled its leaves in the fall of the year,
And whistled and roared in the winter alone,
Is gone,–and the birch in its stead is grown.–
The Knight's bones are dust,
And his good sword rust;–   10
His soul is with the saints, I trust.

(? 1817)

GLOSSARY

Sir Arthur O'Kellyn – the name is made up; there is no
historical Sir Arthur O'Kellyn.
Helvellyn – a mountain in the English Lake District.

QUESTIONS

Analyse the verse form (metrical pattern and rhyme) and
comment on how it affects the tone and meaning of the poem.

165

Why did Coleridge make up the name for the knight, rather than write about a knight who actually lived? (hint – consider the rhyme scheme).

What is the effect of the three rhymed short lines at the end of the poem?

What do the oak and birch trees symbolise?

How can the poem be interpreted as an allegory of human life?

COMMENTARY

The poems is written in an unusual metre consisting of four dactyllic feet (a dactyl is a poetic foot with a sort of waltz rhythm). The effect of the metre is mildly humorous (limericks are written in dactyls), which makes the poem a light hearted reflection on life and death.

The two main symbols in the poems are trees: the oak symbolising strength (ships of the line – battleships – were made of oak in Coleridge's time), and the birch symbolising renewal (it is significant that it is a "young birch tree".

Lines 9 and 10 are short, but together they make up the four dactyllic feet of the previous lines, and the last line is in a different metre altogether; iambic tetrameter. The short lines give emphasis to the to the decay of the knight and his sword, and the different metre of the final line perhaps suggests the doubt that is implied by "I trust". This may not be a religious doubt, but a doubt about whether a man who has fought and killed would be worthy of heaven.

Some commentators take the whole poem as an allegory of human life. However strong a person is, he/she will die and decay, but will be reborn into eternal life, which the birch symbolises.

YOUTH AND AGE

Verse, a breeze mid blossoms straying,
Where Hope clung feeding, like a bee—
Both were mine! Life went a-maying
    With Nature, Hope, and Poesy,
      When I was young!   5

When I was young?—Ah, woful When!
Ah! for the change 'twixt Now and Then!
This breathing house not built with hands,
This body that does me grievous wrong,
O'er aery cliffs and glittering sands,   10
How lightly then it flashed along:—
Like those trim skiffs, unknown of yore,
On winding lakes and rivers wide,
That ask no aid of sail or oar,
That fear no spite of wind or tide!   15
Nought cared this body for wind or weather
When Youth and I lived in't together.

Flowers are lovely; Love is flower-like;
Friendship is a sheltering tree;
O! the joys, that came down shower-like.   20
Of Friendship, Love, and Liberty,
      Ere I was old!

Ere I was old? Ah woful Ere,
Which tells me, Youth's no longer here!
O Youth! for years so many and sweet,   25
'Tis known, that Thou and I were one,
I'll think it but a fond conceit—
It cannot be that Thou art gone!
Thy vesper-bell hath not yet toll'd:—
And thou wert aye a masker bold!   30
What strange disguise hast now put on,
To make believe, that thou art gone?
I see these locks in silvery slips,
This drooping gait, this altered size:
But Spring-tide blossoms on thy lips.   35
And tears take sunshine from thine eyes!
Life is but thought: so think I will
That Youth and I are house-mates still.

Dew-drops are the gems of morning,
But the tears of mournful eve!   40
Where no hope is, life's a warning
That only serves to make us grieve,
        When we are old:

That only serves to make us grieve
With oft and tedious taking-leave,   45
Like some poor nigh-related guest,
That may not rudely be dismist;
Yet hath outstay'd his welcome while,
And tells the jest without the smile.

(1823-1832)

GLOSSARY

a-maying – the celebration of May Day, a feast associated with
    youth and fertility.
Poesy – poetic for 'poetry'.
'twixt – no, not your favourite chocolate bar: short for **betwixt**
    – between.

skiff – a light rowing boat.
ere – before (poetic).
vesper-bell – vespers is a sunset evening prayer service.
aye – poetic for 'forever'.
masker – a person wearing a mask at a masked ball.

QUESTIONS

Analyse the verse form of the poem with a focus on metre, rhyme and the refrain-like short lines.

What did Coleridge most value about his youth?

What words, phrases and images does he use to describe youth?

When he looks in his mirror, what does he see? How does he attempt to cheer himself up, and why does the attempt fail?

What final image does Coleridge leave us with and what is its effect?

Think of three words to describe the tone of this poem and justify your choice.

COMMENTARY

There is an early draft of this poem from 1823 when Coleridge was 51 – hardly old age! However, Coleridge had suffered from ill-health for most of his life, and this was worsened by his opium addiction, so he, no doubt, felt older than his years.

The poem is written in iambic tetrameters with a varied rhyme scheme. Three of the strophes end with short lines of two iambic feet. They are not refrains, because their wording is different, but they have the effect of refrains. The first one emphasising youth, and the other two emphasising age.

The first strophe is a short celebration of Coleridge's youth. He says that he had two wonderful things in his life: poetry and hope.

He begins the next strophe with the question: "When was I young?", and laments the fact that the very question shows that there has been a "change". He recalls the time when his body was as light and lively as a "trim skiff". The metaphor is extended to describe how the skiff "flashed along" lakes and rivers, and had no need of "sail or oar" and no fear of "wind or tide". The strophe ends with the interesting idea of Coleridge and Youth living in his body together.

The next strophe goes on to praise the "Friendship, Love and Liberty" he enjoyed before "ere" he was old. That word, "ere" links to the next strophe, where he calls the word "woful", because it proves that youth has gone. He describes his present appearance in the mirror:

> I see these locks in silvery slips,
> This drooping gait, this altered size...

then cheers himself with the idea that "Life is but a thought" and so he will think that he is still young. However, in the next strophe, he uses the image of dew drops compared to tears to express his grief that there is no hope left in old age.

In the last stanza he seems to lapse into depression with an uncomfortable simile to describe old age: it is like a guest who has "outstay'd his welcome" and his attempts to feel young are like a "jest without the smile". Thus, overall, it is a poem of melancholy reflection.

CONSTANCY TO AN IDEAL OBJECT

Since all that beat about in Nature's range,
Or veer or vanish; why should'st thou remain
The only constant in a world of change,
O yearning Thought! that liv'st but in the brain?
Call to the Hours, that in the distance play,   5
The faery people of the future day—
Fond Thought! not one of all that shining swarm
Will breathe on thee with life-enkindling breath,
Till when, like strangers shelt'ring from a storm,
Hope and Despair meet in the porch of Death!   10
Yet still thou haunt'st me; and though well I see,
She is not thou, and only thou art she,
Still, still as though some dear embodied Good,
Some living Love before my eyes there stood
With answering look a ready ear to lend,   15
I mourn to thee and say–'Ah! loveliest friend!
That this the meed of all my toils might be,
To have a home, an English home, and thee!'
Vain repetition! Home and Thou are one.
The peacefull'st cot, the moon shall shine upon,   20
Lulled by the thrush and wakened by the lark,
Without thee were but a becalméd bark,
Whose Helmsman on an ocean waste and wide
Sits mute and pale his mouldering helm beside.

And art thou nothing? Such thou art, as when   25
The woodman winding westward up the glen
At wintry dawn, where o'er the sheep-track's maze
The viewless snow-mist weaves a glist'ning haze,
Sees full before him, gliding without tread,
An image[456:2] with a glory round its head;   30
The enamoured rustic worships its fair hues,
Nor knows he makes the shadow, he pursues!

(? 1826)

GLOSSARY

veer – turn aside.
faery – 'fairy' - spelled this way to avoid childish associations.
meed – a well-deserved reward
bark – barque – a type of sailing ship.
glen – valley.
rustic – relating to the countryside; rural..

QUESTIONS

Analyse the verse form of the first six lines.

How does Coleridge establish the idea of constancy in the first three lines?

What words, phrases and images reveal the constancy of his love for Sara Hutchinson?

What qualities does he think she "embodies"?

Look at the definition of "meed" in the glossary. Why does he think the things he mentions in line 18, are his meed – in other words, why are they "well deserved"?

Comment on the image that he uses in lines 22-24 to describe how important Sara is to his dream.

The last image is the most powerful in the poem. Read the explanation of the image in the commentary and then, in your own words, say why it is effective.

COMMENTARY

This poem appears to have been written when Coleridge was living in Malta from 1804-1806, though it was not published until much later. The evidence for this is in line 18: "To have a home, an English home, and thee!"" (He world hardly specify 'English' unless he were in a foreign country feeling homsesick).

The "Ideal Object" is Sara Hutchinson, with whom he had fallen in love when he moved to Greta Hall in 1799. She did not return his love, but Coleridge continued to love her for the rest of his life, as is shown in this poem which celebrates his "constancy" to her.

He begins by asking himself the question why she should be "The only constant in a world of change". He continues with the strange image of personified Hope and Despair meeting "at the porch of Death". This reminds us of several poems where Coleridge has written about Hope, and explained his despair at his failure to control his opium addiction and achieve something in his writing, for example, *Dejection: An Ode*. Perhaps he is identifying her with Hope and himself with Despair. He picks up the idea of death in the next line where he uses the metaphor that she still haunts him. She is not dead, or a ghost, but because he still loves her, she is a continuing, invisible presence. Line 12 is puzzling: "She is not thou, and only thou art she" – does he mean that Hope is not Sara, but Sara inspires hope? The rest the poem, fortunately, is clear enough: whether or not she can be identified with hope, she certainly embodies 'Good" and "Love". In line 16, Coleridge can only address her as "loveliest friend" because she did not return his love and they never became lovers. He goes on to state that his highest aspirations are to: To have a home, an English home, and thee!". His description of that home is an English rural idyll: a country cottage "lulled" by the singing of thrush and skylark. This is his ideal home, but he emphasises how empty and "waste" it would be without her with a powerful extended metaphor:

> Without thee were but a becalméd bark,
> Whose Helmsman on an ocean waste and wide
> Sits mute and pale his mouldering helm beside.

This is immediately followed by the most vivid and unusual image in the poem, which is best described in Coleridge's own words from *Aids to Reflection*:

> The phenomenon of the Brocken-spectre... refers to a curious phenomenon which occurs occasionally when the air is filled with fine particles of frozen Snow, constituting an almost invisibly subtle Snow mist, and a person is walking with the Sun behind his back. His shadow is projected, and he sees a figure moving before him with a glory round his head. I have seen it myself twice..."

The last line of the poem explains what he is trying to say with this image: "Nor knows he makes the shadow, he pursues!" In other words, he is aware that the Sara Hutchinson in his mind is, at least in part his own creation, particularly with regard to the qualities he has attributed to her in the poem: Hope, Good and Love.

THEMES

Themes are slippery things as different readers will identify different themes in the same text, or the same themes but will give them different names. After much consideration, the author believes that four main themes can be identified in this selection. Students and teachers are advised to do an online search and make a list of the many different themes that other critics have identified, select those that make sense (many do not!) and prepare students to write about them.

NATURE AND THE SUBLIME

Coleridge, through his philosophical studies (particularly of Kant, and Neo-Platonism), made a great contribution to the philosophy of the Romantic movement, and this can be seen in his poems. Put simply, there is a progression of thought (which is similar in Wordsworth's poetry) along the lines of Nature => the Sublime => Pantheism.

Many of Coleridge's poems express a deep love of nature. For example, his description of his "Cot" in *The Aeolian Harp* and *Reflections on Having Left a Place of Retirement*, the beauty of the Quantock Hills in *Fears in Solitude*, and in many other poems. Indeed, there is hardly a poem (except his gothic poems) which does not contain a description of a beautiful natural scene, and even in his gothic poems there are descriptions of imaginary natural scenes

His descriptions of nature are based on actual experiences of specific scenes at specific times of day, or observations made on walks in the country. For example, in *Fears in Solitude*, Coleridge begins by describing a beautiful place in the Quantock Hills in Somerset. It is "green and silent", except for the lark's "minstrelsy". Alliterating adjectives like, "gay", "gorgeous" and "golden" describe the furze. The sunshine, continuing the alliterative adjectives, "glimmers".

But he goes beyond mere description to suggest that these beautiful scenes have a beneficial influence on us. For example, in *Frost at Midnight* he expresses the belief that his son will have a much better education than he had if he is educated by Nature:

> But *thou*, my babe! shalt wander like a breeze
> By lakes and sandy shores, beneath the crags
> Of ancient mountain, and beneath the clouds...

Many of Coleridge's nature descriptions are of everyday scenes such as his cottage, in *The Aeolian Harp,* and the landscape around it ("yon beanfield"). However, in several descriptions he goes beyond everyday scenes into the realms of the sublime. The sublime in literature is description that excites emotions beyond ordinary experience, for example, description of wild nature or scenes of grandeur. These are best exemplified by the painter, Salvator Rosa, and the nature descriptions in the novels of Anne Radcliffe.

For example, *Fears in Solitude* includes descriptions such as "bleak mount", "bare bleak mountain", "with bushy rocks o'er-browed", "Dim coasts, and cloud-like hills", which are bordering on the sublime, and in Kubla Kahn we see it in the sense of "turbulent Nature" and the "ceaseless turmoil" of the "mighty fountain", and the "mazy motion" of the "sacred river".

The heightened emotions evoked by the sublime ultimately lead to Pantheism – seeing God through Nature, which is a theme in its own right.

QUESTIONS

Find five examples of descriptions of nature in different poems, and analyse them by looking for these points:

- Where is it?
- What is the time of day?
- What emotions does it evoke in the author?
- What words, phrases and figures of speech does Coleridge use to describe the scene?
- What philosophical thoughts are inspired by the scene?

What examples does he give of the beneficial effects of nature on the human spirit?

Re-read the description of the sublime and find examples in Coleridge's poetry. Note whether they are descriptions of real or imaginary scenes.

Compare and contrast Coleridge's nature descriptions with those of Wordsworth (for example, in *Tintern Abbey*), Thomas Grey (for example, *Elegy Written in a Country Churchyard*), and Ann Radcliffe (any nature description from *The Mysteries of Udolpho*).

RELIGION AND PANTHEISM

The sense that nature is beneficient, coupled with the sense of awe inspired by the sublime, leads on to Pantheism. Pantheism is the belief that God is in all things, particularly in Nature (so you don't have to go to church on Sunday – just go for a nature ramble).

In *The Aeolian Harp*, we see an early expression of Coleridge's Pantheistic philosophy:, especially in these lines:

O! the one Life within us and abroad,
Which meets all motion and becomes its soul...

Fears in Solitude contains a much fuller expression of Pantheism. He begins by describing the Quantock Hills and their beneficial effects on the human spirit ("tis a quiet spirit-healing nook") and continues with reflections of a Pantheistic nature:

> And he, with many feelings, many thoughts,
> Made up a meditative joy, and found
> Religious meanings in the forms of Nature!

Coleridge returns to this idea later in the poem:

> All adoration of the God in nature,
> All lovely and all honourable things.
> Whatever makes this mortal spirit feel
> The joy and greatness of its future being?

Reflections of this kind can be found in many other poems. For example, in *Dejection: An Ode*, he describes his sense of

> A light, a glory, a fair luminous cloud
>   Enveloping the Earth—

Coleridge's Pantheism is interwoven with traditional Christianity, and both Wordsworth and Coleridge became more conventional in their religious beliefs as they grew older. An example of traditional Christian beliefs is *The Ancient Mariner*. Although there are superstitious elements in the idea of a bird of ill omen, the Ghost Ship and the Death-in-Life figure, the Mariner cannot be finally released from his curse until he has received Christian confession and absolution. The moral of the poem also has a Christian message:

> He prayeth best, who loveth best
> All things both great and small;
> For the dear God who loveth us,
> He made and loveth all.

Traditional Christian references appear frequently in many other poems. For example, in *Reflections on Having Left a Place of Retirement*, he writes about: "Science, Freedom, and the Truth in Christ" and ends with "Speed it, O Father! Let thy Kingdom come!"

Often, Pantheism and Traditional Christianity are blended, so when, at the end of *Dejection an Ode*, he writes: "And when I rose, I found myself in prayer." We can see this as a response to God in Nature, or a prayer to the traditional Christian God.

QUESTIONS

Collect evidences of the stages of Coleridge's belief in Pantheism:
  1) the beauty of nature
  2) it's beneficial influence
  3) religious elements
  4) the idea that all things are One.

Collect all the references to traditional Christianity, and discuss how far they are compatible with Coleridge's Pantheistic beliefs.

How different might Coleridge Pantheistic beliefs have been if he had experiences nature "red in tooth and claw" in the African Savannah?

GOTHIC, MEDIEVALISM AND ORIENTALISM

Gothic literature includes such motifs as: horror, fear, extreme emotions, the supernatural and romance. It was particularly popular in the novel, a contemporary example being Radcliffe's *The Mysteries of Udolpho* (1794). Many gothic texts were given a medieval setting (*Udolpho* begins in 1584), and the gothic revival in literature was coupled with an interest in gothic architecture, prime examples being Horace Walpole's Strawberry Hill (1749), Ashridge Park, by James Wyatt (1806), and Westminster Palace, by Sir Charles Barry and A.W. Pugin (1834).

The gothic is also related to Orientalism – which was a different source of the strange and exotic. Orientalism was an important movement in the visual arts, architecture and interior design. The

Royal Pavilion at Brighton being the prime example.

At one time, Coleridge worked at correcting the proofs of gothic novels, and perhaps that is how he became interested in the genre. Gothic novels were regarded as sensational reading for ladies of leisure, and not serious works of literature, which is probably the reason that Wordsworth disapproved of Coleridge's gothic poems, *The Ancient Mariner* and *Christabel*.

Though the historical setting of *The Ancient Mariner* is not specified, the archaic language and the mariner's use of a crossbow to shoot the Albatross, and the Hermit suggest a medieval setting. A description of the gothic and horror elements in *The Ancient Mariner* can be found on pages 44-47.

Christabel clearly has a medieval setting established by words such as "castle", "knight" and "palfrey". A description of the gothic and horror elements can be found on pages 80-81.

Kubla Khan is an orientalist poem with a description of a "pleasure dome" reminiscent of the Royal Pavilion in Brighton (see pages 26-27). It also contains elements of gothic horror in descriptions such as "savage", "enchanted", and most extreme of all: "haunted by a woman wailing for her demon-lover!"

It is clear that Coleridge had reservations about this aspect of his work. *The Ancient Mariner*, though it was the first poem in *Lyrical Ballads*, and did much to contribute towards its success, was criticised by Wordsworth. *Christabel* was composed piecemeal over a period of four years and he was unable to finish it. *Kubla Kahn* is just a fragment. If he had believed in this aspect of his work more, and had the encouragement of his friend, Wordsworth, he might have finished the unfinished poems, and even written others of the same kind. It is arguable that the gothic part of his oeuvre is his best work, and if he had had the self-belief necessary to develop it, his stature as a Romantic poet might be even higher than it is today.

QUESTIONS

Research the gothic novel, and find out about attitudes towards the novel in the 18th and early 19th centuries.

In the light of your research why do you think Wordsworth, and even Coleridge himself, undervalued his gothic productions?

How does Coleridge use language to evoke a medieval setting?

Compare the extent to which Coleridge uses archaisms in *The Ancient Mariner* and *Christabel*. Do you think that he over-uses archaism in the former?

Research Orientalism, and examine the Orientalist elements in *Kubla Khan*.

LOVE AND FRIENDSHIP

Coleridge is not a love poet, but there are several poems in which he expresses love for a woman; first his wife, Sara Fricker, for example, in the poem *The Aeolian Harp* which is, in part, a love poem (see page 7). Later, he expresses his love for Sara Hutchinson, most notably in *Dejection: An Ode* (see pages 147-151), and *Constancy to an Ideal Object*.

He also expresses a different kind of love, the love of a parent for a child, in his references to his son Hartley, particularly in *The Nightingale* and *Frost at Midnight*. But it is as a poet of Friendship that he stands out.

The most notable "friendship poem," is *This Lime-Tree Bower My Prison* in which he reflects on the pleasures of friendship that he is missing because his injured foot prevents him from walking with his friends (William and Dorothy Wordsworth, Charles Lamb and his wife, Sara). He imagines himself with them and the thought makes him "glad". He refers to Charles Lamb, to whom the poem is addressed, as "gentle-hearted" no less than three times. The poem shows remarkable qualities of empathy with the feelings of others, that must have made him a very good friend in reallife.

To William Wordsworth expresses praise of his friend's poem, *The Prelude*, and his own humility and self-doubt. He describes Wordsworth as "my comforter and guide". It is a deep expression of an unequal friendship in which Coleridge humbles himself before his friend.

The theme of friendship goes beyond any particular poem, for in all his "conversation poems" he is, in effect, making a friend of the reader. The tone and style – iambic pentameters written in informal language – give the impression that he is inviting the reader into his confidence and chatting to him about his innermost thoughts and feelings. The relaxed style seems bland at first, but we have to appreciate it against the background of elaborate and formal 18th century verse. Indeed, even Wordsworth's later blank verse seems over-elaborate by comparison.

QUESTIONS

Collect references to romantic love in Coleridge's poems, then evaluate him as a love poet. It would be interesting to compare him with Shakespeare, particularly in the sonnets, John Donne, or Byron.

Collect the references to Hartley in Coleridge's poems. What does he have to say about his hopes for his education and development?

Find examples in the conversation poems when the tone and style sounds as though Coleridge is talking informally to a friend.

EXAMINATION QUESTIONS

Trace the development of Coleridge's belief in the influence of nature in the poems in this selection.

A key principle expressed in *The Preface to the Lyrical Ballads* was that poetry should be written "in the language of men". When does Coleridge adhere to this principle and when does he depart from it, and with what effect? Trace his increasing use of poetic diction in his later poems (hint: look at the glossaries).

Coleridge is often described as a "poet of the imagination". Which do you think are his most imaginative poems, and why?

Explain what is meant by the literary term "gothic", and discuss the gothic elements in Coleridge's poetry.

Coleridge wrote "What comes from the heart goes to the heart". What "comes from the heart" in his poetry? What goes to your heart?

"In Coleridge's poetry we can see his exaltation, despair and self-doubt". Discuss.

Coleridge's religious beliefs, as expressed in his poems, are a mixture of Pantheism and traditional Christianity. Explore this dichotomy with reference to the poems in this selection.

Coleridge wrote: "Works of imagination should be written in very plain language; the more purely imaginative they are the more necessary it is to be plain." To what extent did he keep his own advice?

"The evidence of Coleridge's opium abuse can be found in his poetry". How far do you agree with this statement?

Write an account of one of the following themes in Coleridge's poems: the supernatural, nature, friendship, self-doubt, love, hope.

Define Pantheism and give an account of Coleridge's Pantheistic beliefs with reference to the poems in this selection.

Most of Coleridge's nature descriptions are of well-known everyday scenes. Give examples, and compare and contrast them with his description of sublime nature and imaginary nature.

"To be loved is all I need,/ And whom I love, I love indeed." Consider Coleridge as a poet of love and friendship.

In what sense can Coleridge be described as "a poet of friendship"?

Coleridge described poetry as "the best words in the best order". How far can this definition be applied to his poetry.

Coleridge urged "willing suspension of disbelief" in order to enjoy his supernatural poetry. Find examples where this is most in need and explain why. Are there any points where the events are so extreme that he loses all credibility?

Coleridge has exceptional powers of description. Give examples, referring to his use of adjectives, his imagery, and other poetic devices.

BIOGRAPHICAL NOTE

Samuel Taylor Coleridge was born on October 21, 1772, in Devonshire. His father was a vicar of a parish and master of a grammar school. After his father died in 1781, Coleridge attended Christ's Hospital School in London, where he met lifelong friend Charles Lamb.

In 1794, Coleridge met a fellow poet named Robert Southey. They constructed a vision of pantisocracy which involved emigrating to the New World with ten other families to set up a commune on the banks of the Susquehanna River in Pennsylvania. Southey had become engaged to a woman named Edith Fricker, so Coleridge decided to marry another Fricker daughter, Sarah (which he preferred to spell 'Sara'). Coleridge was married in 1795, but his marriage was unhappy and he spent much of it apart from his wife.

In 1795 Coleridge befriended William Wordsworth, who greatly influenced Coleridge's verse. From 1797 to 1798 he lived near Wordsworth and his sister, Dorothy, in Somersetshire. In 1798 the two men collaborated on a joint volume of poetry entitled *Lyrical Ballads*. The collection is considered the first great work of the Romantic school of poetry and begins with Coleridge's poem, *The Rime of the Ancient Mariner*.

That autumn the two poets traveled to the Continent together. Coleridge spent most of the trip in Germany, studying the philosophy of Immanuel Kant, Jakob Boehme, and G. E. Lessing. While there he mastered the German language and began translating. When he returned to England in 1800, he settled with family and friends at Keswick. It was at this time that he fell in love with Wordsworth's wife's sister, Sara Hutchinson. He wrote poetry to her, but she never returned his love.

Over the next two decades Coleridge lectured on literature and philosophy, wrote about religious and political theory. He lived for two years on the island of Malta as a secretary to the governor in an effort to overcome his poor health and his opium addiction.

He died in London on July 25, 1834.

ABOUT THE AUTHOR

Chris Webster read English at St David's, Lampeter, and Leeds University, and is now a teacher and writer. His first educational publication was *Poetry Through Humour and Horror* (Cassell, 1987). This was followed by many more educational publications including books for KS3 and GCSE English Language and Literature, published by Hodder, and the best-selling *100 Literacy Hours* (Scholastic, 1997/2005). More recently he has published study notes on the poetry of *Christina Rossetti* and *Ezra Pound*, which, like this book, arose from his classroom teaching. He has also published several novels, the most recent of which is entitled *Murder at St Cuthbert's: A Commodore 64 Mystery*.